Dynamics of Desktop
Publishing Design

M&T BOOKS

Dynamics of Desktop Publishing Design

For users of PageMaker 3.0

Tony Webster
and
Barbara Larter

From original research by Colin Wheildon

M&T BOOKS

M&T Publishing, Inc.
Redwood City, California

M&T Books
A Division of M&T Publishing, Inc.
501 Galveston Drive
Redwood City, CA 94063

M&T Books
General Manager, Ellen Ablow
Editorial Project Manager, Michelle Hudun
Project Editor, Dave Rosenthal
Editor, Kurt Rosenthal
Cover Designer, Michael Hollister
Cover Photographer, Michael Carr

Printed in the United States of America
First Edition published 1989

Library of Congress Cataloging in Publication Data

Webster, Tony, 1940–
    Dynamics of desktop publishing design.

    Includes index.
    1. Desktop publishing. 2. Printing, Practical--
Layout--Data processing.   I. Larter, Barbara.   II. Title.
Z286.D47W44 1989   686.2'2544536   89-12526

ISBN 1-55851-051-6 $22.95

93 92 91 90 89   5 4 3 2 1

Trademarks

Arts & Letters is a trademark of Computer Support Corp.

AutoCAD™ is a trademark of Autodesk, Inc.

GEM™, GEM Desktop™, GEM Draw™, GEM Paint™, and GEM Graph™ are trademarks of Digital Research Inc.

Headline and Newfont are a trademarks of Corel Systems Corp.

Hercules™ Graphics card is a trademark of Hercules Computer Technology

Hijaak® is a trademark of INSET Systems Inc.

IBM is a registered trademark of the IBM Corp.

LaserJet Series II is a trademark of Hewlett-Packard

LaserWriter is a trademark of Apple Computer, Inc.

Macintosh™ is a registered trademark of Apple Computer, Inc.

Microsoft® Work and Microsoft Windows™ Paint are registered trademarks of Microsoft Corp.

PageMaker® is a trademark of Aldus Corporation

PC Paintbrush™ is a trademark of Z-Soft Corp.

PostScript™ is a trademark of Adobe Systems, Inc.

QMS® is a registered trademark of QMS, Inc.

Limits of Liability and
Disclaimer of Warranty

Acknowledgments

This book is based on major research conducted by Colin Wheildon, Publications Editor for the National Roads and Motorists Association in Sydney, Australia.

It was adapted to desktop publishing by Webster & Associates. We are indebted to initial work also carried out by Susan Tyrrell while working with Co-Cam Computer Services. Tom Scott from Creative Colour also provided many helpful suggestions.

The software used in production was Microsoft Word, Microsoft Paintbrush, Hijaak, Arts and Letters, Tops 2.0, CorelDRAW, XEROX Ventura Publisher 2.0, and PageMaker 3.0. Screen shots were taken on Macintosh monitors and Hercules resolution screens.

Contents

Chapter 1 - The Principles of Graphic Design   1

    Understanding reading patterns 4
    Traditional publishing versus electronic publishing 8
    The Steps in Conventional Publishing 9
    The Steps in Desktop Publishing 10

Chapter 2 - Appropriateness of Design   11

    Designing for a target audience 13
    The audience 13
    The essence of the message 13
    The desired action, if any, that you want the audience to take 14
    Typical example of appropriateness of design 15

Chapter 3 - Getting Started   17

    Planning 19
    Thumbnail sketches 20
    Establish format and page layout 23
    Copy fitting 26
    Master chapter components 28
    Chapter 3 Exercise—Newsletters:
      The Front Page 30

Chapter 4 - Type 37

Different type for different results 39
Headlines 41
Out, damned spot! 43
Headlines, kerning, and condensing 45
Body text 56
Is italic body type as black as it's painted? 58
Ragged right or left, or justified? 59
Widows, jumps, and bastard measure 61
Examples of body text settings 64
PageMaker font capabilities and options 69
Adobe fonts 69
Bitstream 72
Typeface examples 76

Chapter 5 - Guidelines For Newsletters 87

Good and bad examples 91
Chapter 5 Exercise—Newsletters:
   The Inside Pages 97

Chapter 6 - Understanding Proportion 101

Type units 103
Shape and type harmony 104

Chapter 7 - Tone Harmony and Contrast 107

Creating type that "talks" 109
Contrast 112

Chapter 8 - Balance   113

   Easy on the reader 115
   Chapter 8 Exercise—Newsletters: Balance 119
   Sample Newsletter 126
   Text and graphic placeholders 130

Chapter 9 - Guidelines for Press Releases   137

   Chapter 9 Exercise—Guidelines for Press Releases 140
   Setting up a template 141

Chapter 10 - Guidelines for Overhead Transparencies   145

   Good and bad examples 149
   Overhead Transparencies 153

Chapter 11 - Display Headlines   157

   Using attention getters 159
   Breaking headlines 161
   Changing headline widths 163

Chapter 12 - Directing Eye Movement   165

   "Stars" and focal points 167
   Pointing devices 168
   Rotating and flipping images 171
   PageMaker pointing devices 171

Chapter 13 - Illustrations 173

When and where to use illustrations 175
Computer-generated graphics 177
PC Paintbrush (image) 177
CorelDRAW (EPSF Line-art) 178
Macintosh drawing files (PICT) 179

Chapter 14 - Borders and Rules 181

How to use them, when, and where 183
Imported borders 186

Chapter 15 - Guidelines for Books, Manuals, and User Documentation 187

Common attributes 189
PageMaker features for long publications 193

Chapter 16 - Principles of Modern Design 207

Basic principles 209
Movement 211
Headline groups 211
Ornamentation 213
Freedom 213

Chapter 17 - Printing in Color 215

Any color as long as it's black 217

Colored headlines 218
Colored text 220
Text on tinted ground 223
Black on not so black 226
Into reverse 228
Bold and bad 230
Conclusion 230
The best colors to use 231

Chapter 18 - Guidelines for Advertisements   233

Elements of design 235

Chapter 19 - Dealing with Printers   243

Understanding the jargon 245
Finding the right printers 249

Chapter 20 - Brochure Design: A Case Study   251

NRMA Leaflets—How Many Are Read? 253
Executive summary 253
Introduction 257
Method 257
Research 259
Summary of Professor Vogele's Research 267
Recommendations 269
Appendix A—Examples of type sizes 270

Chapter 1
The Principles of Graphic Design

Chapter 1
The Principles of Graphic Design

Newspapers, magazines, newsletters, and professional documents are vehicles for transmitting ideas. Their design is an integral part of the communication process, and forever under scrutiny.

Design is not mere decoration, but part of the business of communication. Good design is a communication mechanism that does not call attention to itself; rather, it leaves the reader aware only of communication and not the mechanism. The focus of good design should not be on the creator's idea of beauty, but on whether those who will read a publication will receive the message intended by the author.

The best print design first captures, and then leads the reader's eye in a smooth, continuous flow called *reading rhythm*. This rhythm can be enhanced or disturbed by the way all the elements comprising the publication—titles, text, pictures, and graphics—are placed.

It is the function of the designer to ensure that these elements work in harmony to encourage reading rhythm and comprehension. If any design or element is out of harmony, it calls attention to itself and competes for the reader's attention.

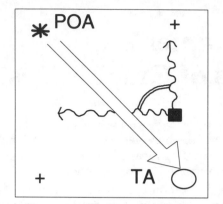

Figure 1.

The Gutenberg Diagram charts basic reading eye movement from the Primary Optical Area (POA) to the Terminal Anchor (TA). Crosses indicate inactive corners, and wavy lines show "backward" movement that the reading eye resists.

Understanding reading patterns

In order to fully understand design skills and typography, a designer must first have a basic knowledge of reading patterns.

When taught to read, we're told to start at the top-left corner of the reading matter and work our way across and down, going from left to right and back again, until we reach the bottom-right corner. The Gutenberg Diagram (Figure 1) defines the reading patterns and design principles that all design should respect.

By habit, the eyes move from the top-left corner, called the *Primary Optical Area* (POA), to the bottom-right corner, called the *Terminal Anchor* (TA). The eyes move down the page, obeying *reading gravity*, and returning after each left-to-right sweep to an *axis of orientation*.

Any design forcing the reader to work against reading gravity, or which fails to return him or her to a logical axis of orientation, tends to destroy the reading rhythm.

Designers must never forget that the people at the other end of the communication process are readers. Readers do not have, as their main aim, the enjoyment of patterns. Rather, their aim is the comprehension of messages. Therefore, designers must support the reader's basic need—to comprehend a message with a minimum of difficulty.

In Figure 6, it can be seen that the eye falls naturally to the headline, then to the introduction, then follows naturally the flow of the body type. The two pieces of half-tone act as magnets to the inactive corners, and the sign-off logotype acts as the terminal anchor.

In Figure 7, instead of being attracted by the headline to the top-left corner, the eyes are attracted by the headline to a point below the upper illustration. Having read the headline, the eyes want to observe the

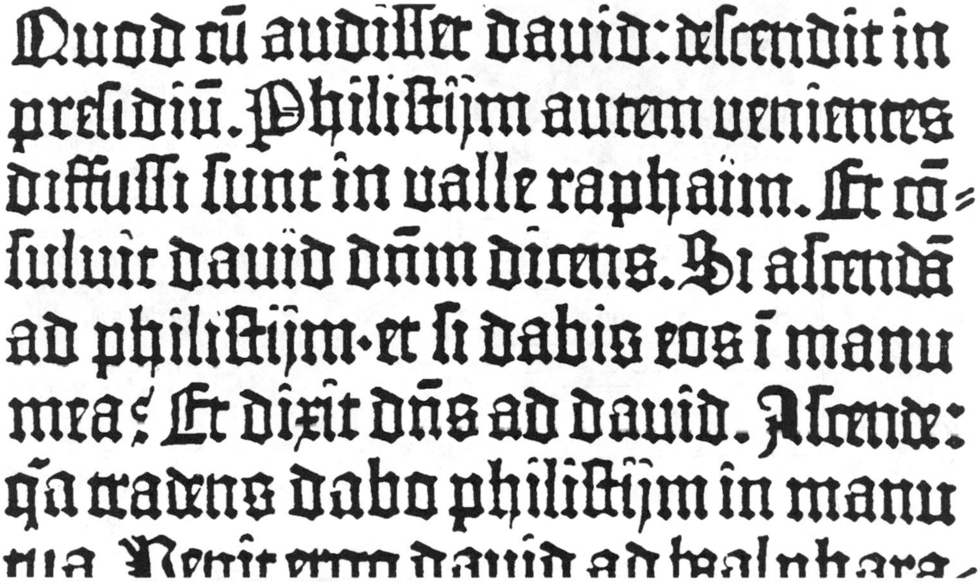

Quod cū audiſſet dauid:deſcendit in preſidiū. Philiſtijm autem venientes diffuſſi ſunt in valle raphaïm. Et cōſuluit dauid dūm dicens. Si aſcendā ad philiſtijm·et ſi dabis eos ī manu mea? Et dixit dūs ad dauid. Aſcende: qa tradens dabo philiſtijm in manu tua. Venit ergo dauid ad baalpharaſ·

Figure 2.
The beginning—an extract from the Gutenberg Bible, 1452-55. Basic reading patterns have not changed.

Figure 3.
An example which follows the Gutenberg diagram.

Figure 4.
A deviation and the reader is easily confused. With the headline in the middle of the text, the reader does not know where to start reading—on the left immediately beneath the headline, or at the top-left of the text itself? Readers will be lost by this simple design error.

Figure 5.
This figure complies with the Gutenberg diagram.

Figure 6.
A defiance of the Gutenberg diagram.

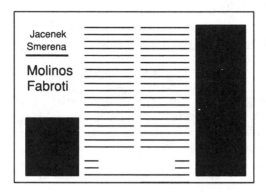

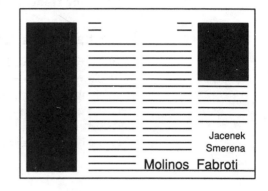

Figure 7.
Another design complying with the principles of reading gravity.

Figure 8.
A design which ignores the rules.

principles of reading gravity and axis of orientation, and fall to the small leg of type in the second column. This obviously will make little or no sense.

The eye is forced to make the journey against reading gravity to the primary optical area to begin the article. The reading rhythm has been lost, and, as research shows, considerable damage may have been done to the reader's comprehension of the article.

Based on research in this area, Table 1 shows the percentages of readers' comprehension levels when matter complies with Gutenberg's principles, and when it does not.

Table 1	Comprehension Level		
	Good	Fair	Poor
	%	%	%
(a) Layout complying with Gutenberg diagram	67	19	14
(b) Layout disregarding Gutenberg diagram	32	30	38

The placement of headlines is critical, but most important are clear starting points to the story. The A.I.D.A (i.e., Attention, Interest, Development, Action) principles in advertising are still a part of maintaining reader contact with context.

Traditional publishing versus electronic publishing

Conventional publishing involves many more steps than electronic or desktop publishing, as shown in Figure 2. Where conventional publishing puts control largely in the hands of "outside" artists, designers, typesetters, and even proofreaders, desktop publishing puts low-cost, high-quality publishing in the hands of the people who previously had to rely on outside specialists.

The Steps in Conventional Publishing

1. Create text. This is generally done on a word processor, and includes the normal steps of entry, proofreading, editing, and correcting the text.

2. Copy sent to typesetter. Copy has to be marked up according to the typesetter's instructions. Type style, size, column width, etc., are some of the instructions that need to be included.

3. Typeset galleys returned from typesetter. These galleys are proofed and errors noted.

4. Corrected galleys sent to typesetter and returned. The marked up galleys are sent to the typesetter for final corrections and printout, and then returned to the customer.

5. Prepare illustrations. Illustrations are prepared using the normal photographic screening process.

6. Page designed. The page layout is sketched out and a final design is arrived at.

7. Paste-up. This is done either in-house, if the facilities exist, or by an outside organization.

8. Necessary changes made. Often extra text needs to be set to fit the page size, or an extra picture sized and screened. Text may need to be sent out to be typeset, proofread, and corrected, as for the initial copy.

9. Final check of layout. A final check of the publication is done just before it is sent for printing. Hopefully, no errors or changes are required. If there are, some of the previous steps may need to be repeated.

The above steps, applied to an eight-page newsletter, generally require about two-weeks. This is an industry average and can occur in less or more time than stated here.

Figure 2 (a).
Conventional publishing steps.

The Steps in Desktop Publishing

1. Create text. As for conventional publishing, this is generally done on a word processor, with the normal steps of entry, proofreading, editing, and correcting the text.

2. Prepare illustrations. This may be done in one of two ways—the normal photographic screening process, or with a scanner. The photographic quality of scanned images is relatively good and improving all the time. Scanners can also be used to help position and crop pictures.

3. Page designed. The page layout is sketched out and a final design is arrived at. This process is more interactive with desktop publishing, as page design can be modified directly on the screen.

4. Format publication. This is the process of electronically laying out the publication on the screen. It is somewhat the same as paste-up for conventional publishing. The flexibility of screen layout far surpasses that of manual layout, however. Desktop publishing allows columns to be changed, type style and size to be modified, and additional pictures included or excluded, much more readily than with the conventional approach.

5. Publication printed out. After any necessary screen changes and modifications, the publication is printed out on a laser printer. Note the major difference here, between the conventional and desktop publishing approaches. With conventional publishing, text hardcopy occurs at the beginning of the process. With desktop publishing, hardcopy only need occur towards the end of the project.

6. Final check of layout. Layout is checked, corrected, and a final version printed out.

The above steps, applied to an eight-page newsletter, generally require around one to two days. This also is an industry standard and may occur in more or less time.

Figure 2 (b).
Electronic publishing steps

Chapter 2
Appropriateness of Design

Chapter 2
Appropriateness of Design

Designing for a target audience

When creating documents, you must first consider these things:

1. *The audience*
2. *The essence of the message*
3. *The desired action, if any, that you want the audience to take*

The selection of design elements should complement the function of the communication.

The audience

It is important to know what your audience is like, and what their needs and objectives are. Some planning and research is needed at this early phase, irrespective of the type of publication you are creating. Creating a document which is wrong for your intended market is very much a total waste of time.

The essence of the message

A product advertisement, for example, should tell readers what benefits they would receive if they purchased the product. Benefits should be communicated as simply and as clearly as possible. Look for unique benefits—ones that competitors can't offer.

A press release, however, should not read like an advertisement. It should contain information of interest to the readers of the publication. Benefits can be mentioned, but should not be emphasized, as they be in an advertisement.

Operator, or How-To manuals should have ample illustrations and a friendly air about them. This is particularly important for manuals that need to be read and understood by relatively non-technical people.

Annual reports in the financial sector should be clear, concise, and straightforward, strongly supported by charts and graphs. The design should also give the feeling of authority, dependability, security, and prosperity.

Newsletters to consumers should be friendly, open, and easy to read. No fine print. They should be supported by photographs and graphics, and have various elements of reader value.

The desired action, if any, that you want the audience to take

What do you want your prospects or customers to do when they read your newsletter, advertisement, press release, etc.?

Advertisements, for example, can have one of a number of objectives. They can:

- *Invite people to send money to buy a product.*

- *Alert people as to the availability of a product or service which is now available as a commercial or consumer item.*

- *Provide brand awareness to keep people loyal to a particular brand.*

- *Provide general information. (This type of advertising is very common for government departments.)*

Newsletters can also be designed for a variety of reasons. They may be used to keep your customers aware of your continuing service or make major new announcements. Newsletters may also include coupons for readers to buy products or services.

Press releases have two audiences. In the first instance, publication editors have to accept and print your release with minimal changes. This requires simple, straightforward facts, double-spaced printing, no "free" advertising, and no more than two pages, in general, per release.

In the second instance, you need to create a desire within the readers of the different publications in which your press release will appear. Make sure your headline clearly identifies the story, and keep the tone business-like.

Typical example of appropriateness of design

To illustrate the above ideas, let us review an example of a computer company, Desktop Computer Systems, producing a monthly newsletter for its customers.

The *target market* could be defined as people who:

1. Are customers of Desktop Computer Systems,

2. Know the company well,

3. Are familiar with the products and the company,

4. And/or are receptive to purchasing more products.

The *message* Desktop Computer Systems would want to get across would be:

- *To enhance company image as a supplier of well-designed computer systems.*

- *To keep customers informed of new product, support, and service offerings.*

- *That it values its customers well enough to keep in regular contact.*

The response could be of two types. One would be more abstract, in which customers would just get a good feeling knowing that Desktop Computer Systems is around, is doing well, and is in the forefront of new computer introductions.

The second, more tangible response would be in the form of customers' responding with orders, or inquiries to meet with sales people to discuss possible orders.

The design of this newsletter would be easy to read, with plenty of product photographs mixed in with the text.

A strong understanding of different customer objectives and needs would be shown, and all product offerings would be positioned to show how they can meet these needs.

The underlying tone would be of confidence in the company's products, and of a company well able to provide state-of-the-art computer systems.

A reader response card should be included.

Chapter 3
Getting Started

Chapter 3
Getting Started

Planning

The first fundamental step in getting started is in planning. Planning involves:

1. *Determining the target market and publication type (Chapter 2).*

2. *Determining the size and scope of the publication, contingent on the size of the budget.*

3. *Gathering together all the elements of the publication, and deciding which element best communicates the subject matter or context. This element will then form the central theme around which the other elements are balanced.*

Point 1 has already been discussed in the previous chapter.

Point 2 would be based upon your target market, message to be presented and budget. These combined factors will determine, for example, on whether you have a four-page or eight-page newsletter, whether it is in color or black and white, and how many copies you may decide to print. As often happens, a compromise is generally required to balance the above factors.

Point 3 looks at the story, diagrams, pictures, graphics etc., which are needed to put together your publication.

Thumbnail sketches

Thumbnail sketches are really just rough hand drawn page layouts in miniature. This is to enable the designer to get a feel for all the elements that need to go into the document, in order to devise a basic design that works - before even turning on the computer.

With desktop publishing, it is easy to experiment with thumbnail sketches on-screen. By using graphic tools from the toolbox, and perhaps some text from example files, it is possible with Page-Maker to move these easily around the screen, and quickly change their appearance if necessary.

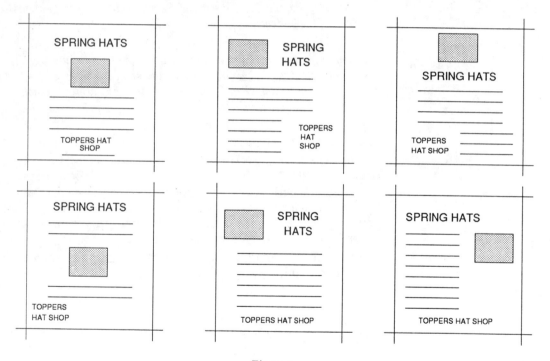

Figure 1.
Draw your thumbnail sketches, then choose the best to enlarge.

Figure 2.
Englarged view of the best thumbnail sketch.

It is therefore good to get into the habit of thumbnail sketches before starting any desktop published document.

First you need to know your page proportions, including your outside margins, - A4, A5, Letter? etc. Then you draw a series of miniature page outlines, say six or seven (Figure 1). Then you begin to put your design ideas into those miniatures. Try drawing your design several ways before deciding on the one that suits your purpose best (Figure 2).

At this stage you should draw a full-size layout, sometimes called a dummy, and transcribe your best thumbnail into it.

Here are a few basic clues in design, based on research, for you to think about.

- *Text within a border will be read before text outside (however, this can be detrimental if the text in the border is a subsidiary part of the article or document).*

- *Vertical shapes are preferred to horizontal shapes, by 80 percent of readers - a diagonal shape is even better.*

- *Captions should be below or to the right of pictures or diagrams.*

- *Numbers stand out more than letters, so if a number is significant, put it in figures, not words.*

- *Color pictures are more appealing than monochrome ones.*

- *Large pictures get attention before small ones.*

- *A sequence of pictures gets attention before individual pictures.*

- *Action pictures will be noted before still pictures.*

- *Pictures of people will be looked at before pictures of products.*

- *Portraits get attention before full length pictures.*

- *Eyes are the first thing focused on.*

- *Children get attention before adults.*

With PageMaker, it is important to establish your format and page layout, and also to determine whether you need to create the document as a template suitable for your application, which can be then used as a 'dummy' for future publications. The following pages of this chapter explore these concepts in more detail.

Establish format and page setup

Components of your template

The use of templates[*] in PageMaker enables document formats to be quickly and easily standardized. The following commands are utilized with this approach:

(i) Page setup (File menu)

- Page Size - Letter, Legal, Tabloid, A4, A3, A5, B5 or select Custom which will allow you to define your own dimensions
- Orientation can be Tall (Portrait) or Wide (Landscape)
- Start page # (1 is always a right hand page and in publications is the accepted standard to begin on this page), and # of pages
- Options of Double-sided and Facing pages are available
- Set the margin dimensions.

```
Page setup                                    ( OK )
Page size:  ○ Letter   ○ Legal   ○ Tabloid    (Cancel)
            ● A4  ○ A3  ○ A5  ○ B5
            ○ Custom:  [210]    x  [297]    mm
Orientation:  ● Tall  ○ Wide
Start page #: [1]     # of pages: [1]
Options:  ⊠ Double-sided   ⊠ Facing pages
Margin in mm:      Inside  [25]       Outside [20]
                   Top     [20]       Bottom  [20]
Target printer: PostScript Printer on LPT2:
```

Figure 3.
The Page Setup dialog box in the File menu.

---

[*] For more discussion on PageMaker templates see *PageMaker 3 By Example,* M&T Books, 1989.

(ii) Column guides (Options menu)
- Choose the number of columns required
- Choose same or different settings for left and right pages
- Define space between columns (gutter width)

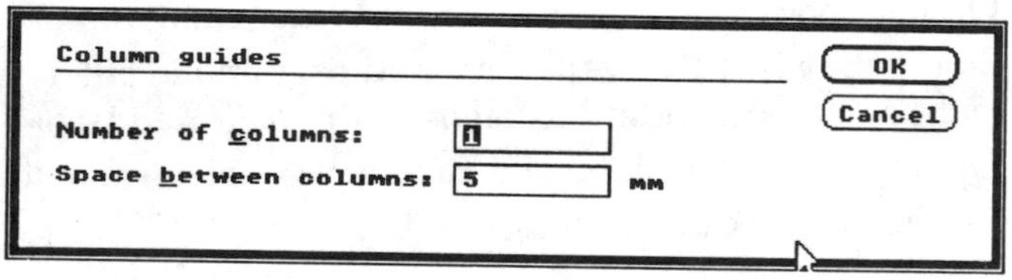

```
┌─────────────────────────────────────────────────┐
│ Column guides                          ( OK )    │
│                                      ( Cancel )  │
│ Number of columns:        [1]                    │
│ Space between columns:    [5]     MM             │
└─────────────────────────────────────────────────┘
```

Figure 4.
The Column guides dialog box in the Options menu.

(iii) Define body text font size and style (Define styles command, Type menu)

Figure 5 shows a page layout, using the above commands, with the following features:

- *Letter*
- *Portrait*
- *Double-Sided*
- *3 Columns*
- *.75" margins (Top, Bottom, Left, Right)*

Any borders or rules can be added to the template by using the toolbox graphics, and defining their attributes in the **Lines** menu.

Guidelines For Newsletters

Newsletters are common methods of communication. They are used to communicate within organizations (as staff newsletters) or to communicate with the outside world (customer newsletters).

Based on the theory already discussed throughout this book, some of the major points to consider when putting together a newsletter are elaborated on below.

Let's consider the first page of, say, a four page newsletter. Important considerations here include (some of which were discussed in Chapter 4):

Don't overdo the Masthead (the newsletter name) or the various story headlines. Within the research undertaken, 57 percent of respondents said they disliked 'screamer headlines'. Sixty-eight percent became bored with long wordy headlines.

Headlines can be serif or sans serif. Studies showed very little difference for readers in this regard.

Don't try to crowd the first page with lots of stories which are all continued on subsequent pages. Sixty-one percent of readers says that these jumps are annoying. Eighty-three percent said they usually disobeyed jumps.

Make sure the headlines are in both upper and lower case.

Apart from the first page, the following major points should be carefully digested:

Keep the body text size appropriate to the audience - at least 10 to 12 point, no smaller.

Have a reasonable amount of graphics and captions. Another important research consideration was that 67 percent

preferred illustrations to carry a caption. Seventy-seven percent said articles in which body type jumped over an illustration was annoying.

Use italics for captions - normally at one point size smaller than the body type.

All body type should be serif not sans serif type (refer back to Chapter 4 where studies showed reader comprehension levels were 67 percent versus 12 percent on serif versus sans serif type).

Use at least two columns per page and preferably three.

Unequal column widths can add variety. For example, if using three-column format, on one page it would be good to run text across two columns. Such stories can often be boxed.

Headers and footers are useful to define such things as page number; newsletter name; and newsletter date.

Double-sided printing is more professional than single-sided.

Consider use of vertical rules between columns. There is no correct yes or no on this, it depends on overall page design.

Special symbols should be used to end stories. This reduces any confusion where multiple stories are contained on one page.

Don't put barriers in the way of body text, particularly if the story continues down the page. Research has shown that once a barrier is reached, the article is expected to continue at the head of the next leg or column.

Good and bad examples

Let's look at some newsletter examples:

Figures 1 to 4 indicate badly designed first pages for the reasons as discussed in the captions. Figures 5 and 6 are acceptable front pages.

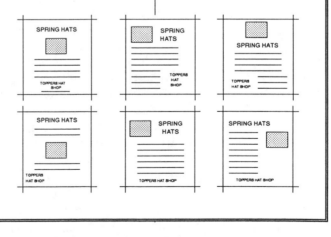

Figure 5.

A standard page layout which can be saved and used for a particular type of publication (e.g. newsletter).

Copy fitting

Copy fitting, in traditional typesetting operations, was never an easy job. You basically needed to count the number of lines, based upon a selected column width and type font, to estimate how much total space would be required. Copy fitting tables, calculations and charts would often be needed to perform this function with reasonable accuracy.

With desktop publishing, however, a whole new world of opportunity opens. Copy fitting can be performed in three different (easier) ways.

Assuming you know how many characters are required per page (or per column), and you are initially entering your text through a standard word processing package, then this package will automatically give you the number of characters in your file. This is the first and simplest method of copy fit. If your text file is too small - add some more; if too large - simply edit it out.

The second method is based upon your word processing package being able to print out in the font type, size and column width required for your final layout. In this case you print out your word processing file, and physically measure it to compare it with the space you have available.

Newer features now becoming available with word processing packages allow WYSIWYG (What-You-See-Is-What-You-Get) page previews of your file in multi-column format. If such packages also allow boxed graphics to be drawn, you can, in effect, preview on the screen your page layout as a word processing file. You can then see, very quickly, whether your copy is too big, too small, or just right. Simple editing at this word processing stage can solve any fit problem that you may have.

The third method of copy fitting is to simply ignore the first two and load your word processing text into PageMaker. Electronically laying the text on screen into a page layout package is, in effect, the latest version of copy fitting. If text doesn't fit, then a number of options are available. These include:

- *Change column width or intercolumn gutter spacing.*
- *Expand or contract the number of pages or columns you require.*
- *Change font type, size, leading etc.*
- *Adjust size and number of pictures.*

In addition, PageMaker's text editing capabilities also allow you to add, delete or modify text directly on screen. This approach of minor text editing on screen is often the simplest, fastest and easiest method of copy fitting.

One final comment. There is a school of thought which says that text may be entered directly into PageMaker, totally bypassing a word processing package. For short amounts of text, this is quite a simple and handy method of working. For large text files, however, we still feel that the initial use of a word processing package is justifiable. The extra capabilities of these programs, including search and replace, spelling checking etc, make their use worthwhile.

PageMaker templates

The components listed above, and illustrated in Figures 3 and 4, have to be determined for each type of publication. These can then be saved as a template and used automatically when required for different types of documents. The template can be as basic or complex as you desire. In addition to the three basic steps outlined, it is quite feasible to define all your paragraph styles at this level, although, remember that each word processing file will bring with it its own defined styles when you load into PageMaker. It's really up to the user to determine which is the easiest procedure to follow.

The type of information which can be included in such a template includes the Masthead (the name of a monthly newsletter, for example), company logo, headers and footers, and areas set aside for graphics. The headers and footers would include constant text such as the publication title, the page number and space for the date (which would be updated on a regular basis).

The master pages are very useful for any information that is repeated on each page. For example headers and footers, page numbers etc. If you have a requirement to have, say, 3 columns on each page throughout your publication or newsletter, these can also be set when you are in the master pages view. You can, at any time alter the columns on individual pages if you so desire.

Figure 6 is an example of a PageMaker template which has been set up for use as a monthly newsletter. The first page shows the company masthead and the position of a rectangle at the bottom left hand page to list the newsletter contents.

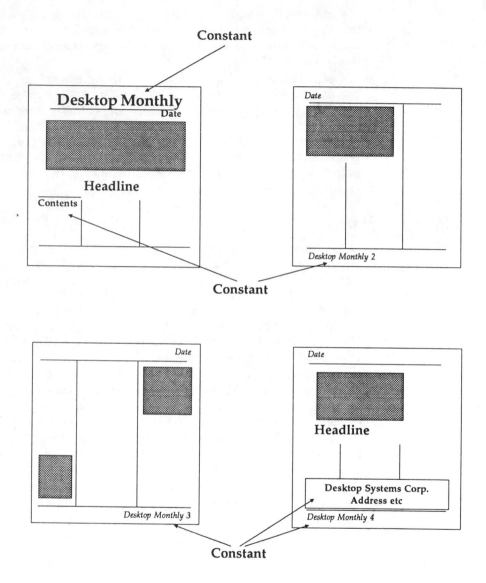

Figure 6.
A four page newsletter dummy or template. With each issue, this template would be opened as a new, untitled version. Note the constant information on the different pages.

Pages two and three are used for general layout, where text and graphics may be mixed in any order, and may vary from month to month. The newsletter title and page number are shown as footers and would be constant for each issue. The header is positioned correctly to include the date - obviously a variable piece of text each month.

On page four, the top two-thirds of the page is free to accept any mixture of text and graphics. The bottom one-third includes standard company information - name, logo, address and phone numbers - which remains constant with each issue.

It is obvious to see that the PageMaker template concept is a much faster way of producing a monthly newsletter, than reproducing all the constant text and graphics each month. A new, untitled copy of the template is opened and then saved with a new name. The template is not changed at all with this approach, and is ready for use again with the next issue.

As an exercise we will now go through the steps of producing the front page of a newsletter, similar to Figure 6.

Chapter 3 Exercise

Newsletters: The Front Page

This exercise is designed to set up the front page of a newsletter suitable for repetitive use on a monthly basis. A reduced view of the suggested front page is shown in Figure 7. We will be setting up pages 2, 3, and 4 of this newsletter in the Chapter 5 exercise. The layout is based on the design principles discussed in Chapters 1, 2, and 3.

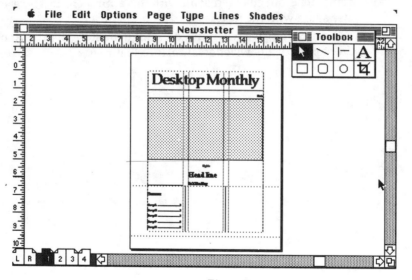

Figure 7.
We are producing a front page design similar to the one illustrated here.

Before starting this exercise you need to begin with a new, untitled document. We are going to establish a PageMaker newsletter template, which we could then use on an ongoing basis for a monthly newsletter design.

Save this document as "Newsletter" and select Template instead of Publication, as is done by default. For the first page, set up the specifications as follows:

(i)Letter page size and four pages long. Select Double-sided and Facing pages options

(ii)Margins of 1.00 inch all around

(iii)Go to Master Pages and set three columns with 0.3 inch (gutter width) for both pages (*Column guides* under the **Options** menu)

(iv)Position the zero axis where the top and left margins cross (on the left master page)

(v)Create the Newsletter title, *Desktop Monthly*, on the first page. Create a paragraph style for this title, which we have called Masthead. Make the Font 60 point Times (Dutch), Bold, and centered. This will not fit (and is not meant to) in the first column (Figure 8). Drag this block of text so it snaps to the

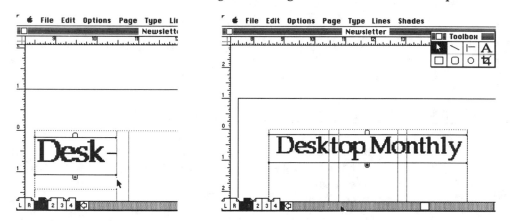

Figure 8.

Once the Masthead has been created, drag the block of text so that it fits between the left and right margins.

outside margins (Figure 8).

(vi)Draw a horizontal, 2-point line of margin width, directly below the title.

(vii) Create the Date so that it sits just below the 2-point line (Figure 9). Define a new style with the Font set at 14 point Times (Dutch), Bold, and Right Justified.

(viii) Create the large picture frame (Figure 9). Use the rectangle tool and begin the frame to the left of the screen and just below the date line. Extend it halfway down the page. The picture frame in Figure 9 begins at 1.5 inch and finishes at 5 inches. The frame has a 10% black background (to illustrate a picture).

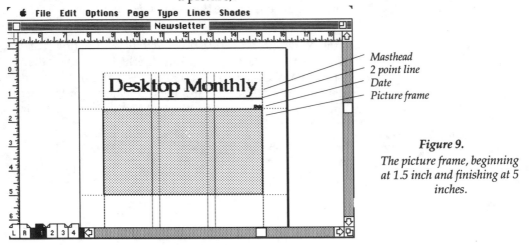

Masthead
2 point line
Date
Picture frame

Figure 9.
The picture frame, beginning at 1.5 inch and finishing at 5 inches.

(ix) Type the word "caption" just below the picture frame and give it a paragraph style (we have called ours Caption) with the following attributes:
Times (Dutch), 10 point, Italic, and Centered.
Again, to resize the caption block to fit across the width of the page, simply drag it to fit.

(x) Type in Headline and Sub Heading as shown in Figure 11 (separated by a return) and apply two more paragraph styles, (we have called them Headline and Subhead). The attributes for Headline should be 30 point, Times (Dutch), Bold, and Left Justified. The attributes for Subhead should be 18 point, Times (Dutch), Bold and Left Justified. If you base these styles on the Body Text style you will need, for the both Headline and Subhead, to insert space after in the Para dialog box—0.1 inch is what we have used.

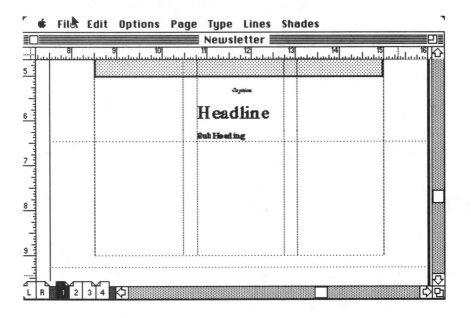

Paragraph specifications _____ (**OK**)

Hyphenation: ☐ Auto ☐ Prompted (Cancel)

Pair kerning: ☒ Auto above `12` points

Alignment: ⦿ Left ○ Right ○ Center ○ Justify

Indents: **Spacing:**

Left:	`0`	inches	Before:	`0`	inches
First:	`0`	inches	After:	`0.1`	inches
Right:	`0`	inches

Figure 10.
The Headline and Subhead styles both have Spacing After set at 0.1 inch.

After creating these two single-line paragraphs, position them in the center column just below the picture frame. In our example of Figure 11, Sub Heading is positioned at 6.5 inches.

⬤ File Edit Options Page Type Lines Shades

Newsletter

Headline

Sub Heading

Figure 11.
The Headline and Sub Heading paragraphs are keyed in and applied the correct paragraph styles.

(xi) Create Contents

Create the Contents information similar to that shown in Figure 12. Situate this block of text in the lower-left corner, column wide. The attributes of the Contents paragraph style should be Times (Dutch), 12 point, Bold, with a right leader tab set at 1.9 inch (leave leading at auto). Type in the information shown in Figure 12. Create a 2-point line 1/2 inch above Contents heading.

You have now created all the styles you need for the front page of your newsletter.

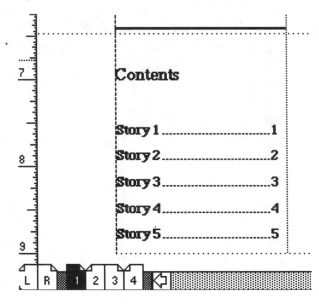

Figure 12.
An enlarged view of the bottom-left hand of the page illustrating the Contents information. We have applied a 14 point font size to the word Contents, although the paragraph style throughout this text is the same.

The final decision is whether or not you wish to have intercolumn rules. Because there are pictures on most pages, the vertical rules are simple to add at any time in PageMaker. In Figure 13 we have included two vertical rules of 1 point thickness. These will be used for the first two columns of text we will place in a further exercise.

Your first page of the Newsletter is now complete and should look similar to Figure 13 below.

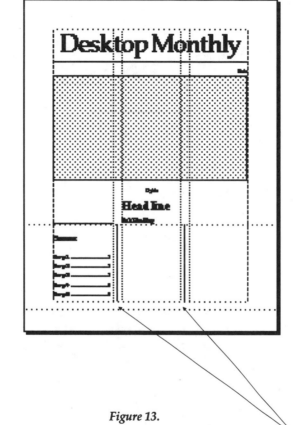

Figure 13.
A screen shot of the completed first page.
Note that we have added two vertical rules in the bottom-third of the page.

Chapter 4
Type

Chapter 4
Type

Different type for different results

When studying the craft of typography, it is appropriate that we start by looking at *type*. Type is nothing more than a mechanical way of producing the alphabet. Desktop publishing type is much more flexible in style than typewriter or word processor type—but that's the only major difference, we are still working with the same 26 letters of the alphabet.

There are a considerable number of kinds of type, and there are some rules and recommendations to cover the basic forms and their best uses.

- **Roman.** These typefaces have serifs, which are small ticks at terminals of letters, and distinguishable thick and thin strokes. There are two basic forms of Roman: *old style*, which has tapered or rounded serifs, and minimal difference between thick and thin strokes; and *modern,* a name which serves only to distinguish it from the old style, with flat serifs and considerable difference between thick and thin strokes.

- **Square Serif**. Also called Egyptian or slab serif, this style has little difference between thick and thin strokes, and heavy slab-like serifs.

- **Sans Serif.** This group is recognizable by the absence of serifs and generally by the uniformity of stroke thickness. Some sans serif faces have variation in the thickness of strokes to aid legibility. These are known as *optically designed* types. Others have uniform strokes, and are called *geometrically designed* type.

- **Script.** Type designed in the style of handwriting.

- **Ornamental**. Examples are Old English and computer styles.

Using several different styles in a document is universally difficult to read because the variety of type designs distracts the reader's attention, and diverts his or her thoughts away from the text to be read and comprehended.

A *typeface* is the design of a certain alphabet. Century is a typeface. A type *font* is one particular alphabet. Century, Bold, Italic, 36 Point is a type font.

A type family refers to all of the fonts, in varying styles of one face. For example, Century Schoolbook, Roman, Bold, Light, Italic are members of the Century family.

Palatino serif font

Avant Garde sans serif font

Zapf Chancery

Figure 1.
Examples of serif, sans serif, and script fonts.

Headlines

Every one of your publications has a message to give to your target audience, and you should give it to them right away. Put it in the headline.

Why? Because research has shown that five times as many people will read the headline as the rest of the publication.

Research has also shown that clever headlines, puns, literary allusions, and snappy words don't work. Here is an example:

In the Australian state of Victoria, a leaflet on random breath testing had the headline **Random breath testing: don't blow your license.** A similar campaign in the state of New South Wales carried the snappy slogan **Don't blow it**. Research showed that all of the people who read the Victorian leaflet would have understood the headline's message, whereas only four percent were aware of the message on the NSW headline. Keep this in mind.

Now we're clear on the message, let's consider the type. There are really two choices: capitals or lowercase.

Lowercase is more legible. Capitals give more authority and distinction. So consider the message—if it's simple and straightforward, you can set it in capitals without a worry. However, if it's complex, or long, use lowercase.

There is little difference between type styles for headlines. It rests largely with the style of the layout and the nature of the publication. There is one point to remember—don't set ornamental letters entirely in capitals.

To give you more food for thought on headlines, see Table 1 on the following page, which summarizes research on some popular type styles. It indicates percentage legibility of the various styles.

Table 1: Legibility of headline styles	%
1. Roman old style lowercase	92
2. Sans serif lower case	90
3. Roman modern lowercase	89
4. Roman old style italic lowercase	86
5. Roman modern italic lowercase	86
6. Sans serif italic lowercase	86
7. Optima lowercase	85
8. Optima italic lowercase	80
9. Roman modern capitals	71
10. Roman old style capitals	69
11. Square serif lowercase	64
12. Roman modern italic capitals	63
13. Roman old style capitals	62
14. Sans serif italic capitals	59
15. Optima italic capitals	57
16. Sans serif capitals	57
17. Optima capitals	56
18. Square serif capitals	44
19. Cursive or script lowercase	37
20.* Ornamented lowercase	24-32
21. Cursive or script capitals	26
22.* Ornamented capitals	11-19
23. Black letter lowercase	10
24. Black letter capitals	3

*The ornamented faces come in various forms, and a range of responses is given.

The difference in perceived legibility between capitals and lower-case of the same type family is significant, as a few examples will show:

	Capitals	Lower case
	%	%
Roman old style	69	92
Roman modern	71	89
Sans serif	57	90
Optima	56	85
Square serif	44	64

Out, damned spot!

Many advertising typographers place a period at the end of their headings. Newspaper typographers tend not to.

The thinking is that editorial headlines in newspapers and magazines rarely form sentences, and therefore don't need periods, but advertising headlines frequently form sentences, and therefore require periods.

To find whether the period has an effect on readers' comprehension, and if that effect is significant, a project was conducted in Sydney between December, 1986, and March, 1987.

Magazine pages were created in the Ayers No. 1 format—slightly less than half-page horizontal illustration, with a headline below it, and the text below again. Four different pages were printed, with each design being in two formats—the headline with a period, and the headline without.

The sample group for each numbered 220. Methodology was to present readers with one page, and ask them to read it in a specific time. Questions were asked about the content of the material to determine comprehension levels. The sample was divided into two groups of 110, each group being given one of the two styles. Later, using a different design, the roles were reversed—the group which had been given the headline with a period first, then received a page headlined without a period. The process was alternated until all four designs had been tested. The sample members were not made aware of the reasons for the tests.

The content of two of the designs was editorial, with a tourism theme. The other two dealt with advertising, with a motoring theme.

There were no significant differences between the individual designs in levels of comprehension. There were, however, differences in comprehension between the headlines with periods and those without periods. The average over the four tests was:

	Comprehension Level		
	Good	Fair	Poor
Headline without period	71	19	10
Headline with period	58	22	20

After the project was completed, the members of the sample were questioned on their reactions to the material. Those who read the headlines with periods were conscious of the punctuation mark, and commented on it.

Twenty-two percent of the total sample said they realized they were reading an advertisement when they came to the period, even though they were not aware of the content at that point. Two percent of the sample indicated this discovery diminished their intention to concentrate on reading the material.

Twelve percent of the sample indicated that they found the use of the periods unnatural, and wondered why they had been used. Six percent of the sample said the period indicated to them that there was no need to read any more of the message. All that needed to be said had been said.

Conclusion: The use of periods at the end of headlines in advertisements has a detrimental effect on readers' comprehension. In the project, thirteen percent fewer readers displayed good comprehension when periods were used. Reasons for this were:

- *The period tends to pull some readers up with a jerk, and indicate to them there is no need to read on.*

- *The period is, to some readers, an indication that what follows is advertising material, and, in their minds, not as consequential as if it were editorial.*

Only two percent of the sample were aware of the subtle distinction that editorial headlines rarely include verbs, and that advertising headlines frequently do.

Headlines, kerning, and condensing

Back in the good old days of hot metal, when everything typographic was ordered and uncomplicated, type came in four basic widths—expanded, natural, condensed, and extra condensed.

But now, with digitized typesetting, photocomposition, and data processing, literally anything goes. Type can be expanded, condensed, stretched, or squeezed to suit the designer's or typesetter's imagination.

The typesetter can make a headline fit around corners, squeeze it into half its original length, or italicize or backslant until the letters fall over.

Anything can be done to bolster the designer's genius, or perhaps to accomodate the headline writer's inability to write a headline that fits.

But should technology serve only the designer and headline writer, or should it also serve the reader? Are we, by distorting type, discomforting the reader to such an extent that he/she will retaliate by refusing to read our message?

If this danger is real, how far can we go before our use of the technology available to us becomes counterproductive.

The possibilities are vast. But regrettably, this typographical horn of plenty contains some questionable fruit.

Kerning is one of these, *condensing* is another. Let's look at kerning first.

Kerning: A *kern* in the days of hot metal or hand-set type was that part of a type letter which protruded above, below, or to the side of the type body, e.g., the curved finial of the letter f. Now in desktop publishing and photocomposition, it gives the operator the ability to control precisely interletter spacing less than that of natural setting.

With kerning, individual letters such as A and W can be closed up to the adjoining letter to obtain optically-even letter spacing.

It's difficult to discern whether kerning is used for aesthetic reasons, or because the headline writer wants another letter space or so without having to use a condensed face or a smaller font. In most instances it appears to be purely for effect.

As more kerning units are employed, the danger increases that letters might become welded together.

It must be asked whether kerning has an effect on type comprehensibility, and at what stage does the effect begin?

To test this, two types were chosen from those families which registered highest in the headline legibility test. The types, Times Roman and Helvetica, were set in 36 point capitals and lowercase, bold, set naturally, and kerned one, two, three, and four units.

The test procedure was identical to the previous headline legibility test.

The test showed that one unit kerning had little effect on legibility. It decreased legibility in serif type, and increased it in sans serif, but minimally on each occasion.

Kerning two and three units has a much more pronounced effect, particularly on the legibility of serif type.

But kern four units, or to the stage where letters merge, and the reader is in dire trouble.

Compounding the problem is that with multiple deck headlines, often the interlinear space is also kerned, and the ascending letters on lower lines merge with the descending letters in the line above. It's when letters merge that the reader cries hold.

Not one reader in the study indicated that headlines in which the letters merged were easy to read. The comprehension level was zero.

It's important to consider the medium on which the work is to be printed. A headline kerned three units may look fine on a photomechanical transfer, but if it is to be printed on newsprint by a coldset press, ink absorption could cause the letters to bleed into one another.

AWAY

(a) Unkerned text.

AWAY

(b) Kerned text.

(c) Normal text.

GoodMorning

(d) Condensed text.

Figure 2.
Examples of kerned and condensed text.

Table 2 shows the relative legibility of headlines set natural and kerned. The figures indicate the positive response as a percentage of the total reader sample.

Table 2

Times Roman: Lowercase	%	Capitals	%
natural	93	natural	68
kerned one unit	92	kerned one unit	66
two units	67	two units	53
three units	44	three units	41
four units	0	four units	0

Helvetica Bold: Lowercase	%	Capitals	%
natural	92	natural	55
kerned one unit	93	kerned one unit	56
two units	79	two units	48
three units	74	three units	44
four units	0	four units	0

Condensing: As well as kerning, headlines can be also condensed to fit into smaller spaces. As an example, a 30 point headline can be squeezed to fit into space taken up by say, an equivalent 24 point headline. This is not done by reducing interletter spacing, as discussed above for kerning, but by actually condensing the text itself.

Let's now look at our research study on condensing, conducted in Sydney in the winter of 1986.

In it, 500 people, balanced by gender, formed a sample, and were asked to read a series of headlines set in four styles: 30 point Univers capitals; 30 point Univers lowercase; 30 point Century capitals; and 30 point Century lowercase.

The headlines were presented set natural, and condensed gradually by single-point increments to the point where the head-line had a width equivalent to 10 point type in the same face, while maintaining its 30 point height.

Readers were asked to indicate:

- *The threshold of condensing at which type became difficult to read.*

- *The type width at which the type was easiest to read.*

- *The style (capitals or lowercase, serif or sans serif) and width of those types shown, which the sample deemed easiest to read.*

The findings are presented below in tabulated form for ease of discussion.

Table 3. The point at which headlines, when condensed, become difficult to read.

Table 3 (a): 30 Point Univers capitals

Width equivalent in points (30 pt base)	Percentage of sample nominating threshold %
23	3
22	19
21 (70% of natural width)	39
20	24
19	8
18 (60 % of natural width)	2
17	4

Two points emerge: 39 percent nominated 21 point as the threshold of difficulty, and 82 percent were within one point of this threshold. Similar results applied to other type styles.

Table 3 (b): 30 Point Univers lowercase

Width equivalent in points (30 pt base)	Percentage of sample nominating threshold %
23	3
22	20
21 (70% of natural width)	39
20	25
19	9
18 (60% of natural width)	2
17	2

Table 3 (c): 30 point Century capitals

Width equivalent in points (30 pt base)	Percentage of sample nominating threshold %
23	2
22	23
21 (70% of natural width)	40
20	22
19	7
18 (60% of natural width)	1
17	1

Table 3 (d): 30 point Century lowercase

Width equivalent in points (30 pt base)	Percentage of sample nominating threshold %
23	4
22	21
21 (70% of natural width)	39
20	22
19	6
18 (60% of natural width)	2
17	1

Table 4. The point of condensing at which headline type is easiest to read.

Table 4 (a): 30 Point Univers capitals

Width equivalent in points	Percentage of sample nominating each width %
30 point (natural width) 7	
29 6	
28 20	
27 (90% of natural width) 40	
26 17	
25 5	
24 (80% of natural width) 3	

Forty percent of the sample indicated headlines condensed by 10 percent (27 point width on 30 point body) were easiest to read, and 77 percent of the sample nominated to within one point of 27 points.

Similar results applied in other type styles.

Table 4 (b): 30 Point Univers lowercase

Width equivalent in points	Percentage of sample nominating each width %
30 point (natural width) 7	
29 6	
28 23	
27 (90% of natural width) 41	
26 14	
25 4	
24 (80% of natural width) 2	

Table 4 (c): 30 Point Century capitals

Width equivalent in points	Percentage of sample nominating each width %
30 point (natural width)	7
29	4
28	25
27 (90% natural width)	43
26	10
25	5
24 (80% of natural width)	3

Table 4 (d): 30 Point Century lowercase

Width equivalent in points	Percentage of sample nominating each width %
30 point (natural width)	6
29	4
28	27
27 (90% of natural width)	37
26	15
25	7
24 (80% of natural width)	3

Table 5. As a check, each member of the sample was shown headlines condensed in increments of three points, and was asked: do you find this style easy to read? Results tended to support the indication in Table 4—that a light condensing makes letter forms easier to read than natural setting in the styles chosen for the test.

Table 5 details are as follows:

Table 5 (a): Univers capitals

Headlines condensed in 3-point increments	Sample nominating style as easy to read %
30 (natural setting)	90
27 (90% of width)	100
24 (80% of width)	94
21 (70% of width)	58
18 (60% of width)	31
15 (50% of width)	0
12 (40% of width)	0

Table 5 (b): Univers lowercase

Headlines condensed in 3-point increments	Sample nominating style as easy to read %
30 (natural setting)	95
27 (90% of width)	100
24 (80% of width)	88
21 (70% of width)	59
18 (60% of width)	33
15 (50% of width)	0
12 (40% of width)	0

Table 5 (c): 30 Point Century capitals

Headlines condensed in 3-point increments	Sample nominating style as easy to read
	%
30 (natural setting)	92
27 (90% of width)	100
24 (80% of width)	84
21 (70% of width)	51
18 (60% of width)	26
15 (50% of width)	0
12 (40% of width)	0

Table 5 (d): 30 Point Century lowercase

Headlines condensed in 3-point increments	Sample nominating style as easy to read
	%
30 (natural setting)	97
27 (90% of width)	100
24 (80% of width)	82
21 (70% of width)	44
18 (60% of width)	28
15 (50% of width)	0
12 (40% of width)	0

Table 6. The sample was asked to indicate which style of setting, including typeface, was easiest to read. The question was asked of Univers, of Century, and of either.

The results are as follows.

Style of setting	Sample nominating as easy to read %
(a) Univers	
Univers lowercase 27	30
Univers lowercase 30	22
Univers lowercase 24	14
Univers capitals 27	13
Univers capitals 24	13
Univers capitals 30	8
(b) Century	
Century lowercase 27	33
Century lowercase 30	21
Century lowercase 24	12
Century capitals 27	12
Century capitals 30	11
Century capitals 24	11
(c) Style of setting, including choice of type face—Univers or Century	
Univers lowercase 27	30
Century lowercase 27	30
Century lowercase 30	22
Univers lowercase 24	11
Univers lowercase 30	7

Summary of Condensing:

1. The point at which headlines, when condensed, become difficult to read appears to be at 70% of natural width. About 39 percent of the sample indicated this point, and a further 44 percent indicated the threshold at 3 percent above or below this width. This result applied to all styles shown to members of the sample.

2. The point of condensing at which headlines were deemed easiest to read was at 90 percent of natural setting. About 40 percent of the sample indicated this, with a similar percentage nominating a width 3 percent above or below the 90 percent width.

3. The style of headline setting deemed easiest to read was lowercase condensed to 90 percent of natural width, with no difference noted between sans serif and serif headlines. Where a choice of type was offered, all participants deemed lowercase easier to read than capitals. This confirms previous research, contained elsewhere within this book.

Body text

There are some hard and fast rules in body text legibility. This is the main bearer of your important message, and comprehension on the part of the reader is of maximum importance.

Text must never be set in volume in sans serif type (i.e., Helvetica). Sans serif is difficult to read in other than small volumes. However, it is ideal for captions and tabulated matter, such as accounts. Serif type is generally easy to read as text. Table 7 shows research results on this point.

Table 7	Comprehension Level		
	Good	**Fair**	**Poor**
	%	%	%
(a) Layout with serif body type	67	19	14
(b) Layout with sans serif body type	12	23	65

Comments made by readers who showed poor comprehension of articles set in sans serif had a common theme—the difficulty in holding concentration.

An analysis of the comments offered by one group of 112 readers who read an article of direct interest follows. Of the 112 readers, 67 showed poor comprehension, and of these:

- *53 complained strongly about difficulties of reading type.*

- *11 said that the task caused them physical discomfort (eye tiredness).*

- *32 said that the type was merely hard to read.*

- *10 said they found they had to backtrack continually to try and maintain concentration.*

- *5 said when they had to backtrack to recall points made in the article they gave up trying to concentrate.*

- *22 said they had difficulty in focusing on the type after having read a dozen or so lines.*

Some readers made two or more of the above comments. Yet when this same group was asked immediately afterwards to read another article with a domestic theme, but set in Corona, they reported no physical difficulties, and no need to recapitulate to maintain concentration.

The conclusion is that body type must be set in serif type for maximum readability and reader comprehension.

The length of lines of text type is also limited by the parameters of legibility. Research has shown that the average human eye can cope with text type of about forty characters in a line. The maximum is about sixty characters, the minimum about thirty characters. Any less than the minimum, any more than the maximum, and fatigue may quickly set into the reader's eyes.

Never set text in capitals. It is common to set speeches in capitals on the assumption that they are easy to read. This is a fallacy.

TRY READING THIS PARAGRAPH, SET IN CAPITAL LETTERS. THE EYES ARE SLOWED AS THEY STRUGGLE TO IDENTIFY LETTERS, AND THEN WORDS AND PHRASES. COMPREHENSIBILITY IS CONSEQUENTLY SLOWED TO A RATE LESS THAN THE READER'S NORM, AND FATIGUE SETS IN.

If this paragraph were set in lowercase the eye would be able to gather in bigger groups of letters and words more easily; comprehension would be faster and better, and with less danger of fatigue.

Be careful setting body text in reverse—white letters on a black background—it can be difficult to read on many occasions.

Kerning should only be used sparingly in body text. Its main function is for large headlines where certain letters look "spacey."

Is italic body type as black as it's painted?

Editors throughout the western world have clung to the proposition that italic body type is illegible, as though it were Holy Writ. There is, however, no reason why it should be true. Italic letters do not offend by any lack of distinction compared to their Roman counterparts.

Serif italics have the same thick and thin strokes, the same height as their vertical fellows, and (possibly a virtue) they slope in the direction of reading.

True, some italic faces have elaborate swashes on some letters; this study was confined to those faces with minimal elaboration to the italic version of the face.

What then, has brought italic body type into such disrepute? It is difficult to see.

It is not the intention to advocate widespread use of italic type as body matter—merely to act as devil's advocate for a style of type which this analysis shows to be wrongly castigated.

A test program was set up with a procedure identical to that for other tests; the body types used were Corona Light Roman and Corona Light italic, 8 on 9 point.

Readers' comments indicated that while italic type caused an initial reaction, because it was unusual in such volume, it caused no difficulty for the reader.

Table 8 shows the comprehension level of italic body type.

Table 8	Comprehension level		
	Good	Fair	Poor
	%	%	%
(a) Layout using Corona Roman text	67	19	14
(b) Layout using Corona Italic text	65	19	16

Ragged right or left, or justified?

Ragged right setting was popularized by the designer Eric Gill in 1930 to eliminate the need (in book setting) for uneven spacings to fill out lines. There's some logic in this, even though the impact on the reader of the unaesthetic spacing may be questionable.

But there's very little logic in ragged right's sinister offspring, that of ragged left setting.

There are those who argue that, for legibility, all body type must be justified completely, as for this book.

Some accept type which is unjustified or ragged at the right, and some magazine and advertising companies occasionally set body matter ragged left.

Many type practitioners will allow ragged right setting yet steadfastly oppose ragged left. Those who accept ragged left setting usually accept both forms.

To test this element, papers were presented with totally justified setting, ragged right and ragged left. It should be mentioned that setting had to be modified slightly to cater for the additional space required to accommodate ragged setting, and that the results apply to complete pages set ragged. The findings may not be entirely appropriate to small amounts of ragged setting.

No matter how much we see, we are never satisfied; no matter how much we hear, we are never content, so I say that
there is nothing better for people than that they should be
happy in their work, for that is what they are here for, and
no one can bring them back to life to enjoy what will be in
the future, so let them enjoy it now.

(a) Ragged left

No matter how much we see, we are never satisfied; no matter how much we hear, we are never content, so I say that
there is nothing better for people than that they should be
happy in their work, for that is what they are here for, and
no one can bring them back to life to enjoy what will be in
the future, so let them enjoy it now.

(b) Ragged right

No matter how much we see, we are never satisfied; no matter
how much we hear, we are never content, so I say that there is
nothing better for people than that they should be happy in
their work, for that is what they are here for, and no one can
bring them back to life to enjoy what will be in the future, so
let them enjoy it now.

(c) Justified

No matter how much we see, we are never satisfied; no matter how much we hear, we are never content, so I say that
there is nothing better for people than that they should be
happy in their work, for that is what they are here for, and
no one can bring them back to life to enjoy what will be in
the future, so let them enjoy it now.

(d) Centered

Figure 3.
Examples of ragged left, ragged right, justified, and centered settings.

Type used was Corona Roman, 8 point on 8.5 point body, and the layout was identical to those used in tests on page design, such as Figure 6 of Chapter 1.

Comprehension levels are shown in Table 9.

Table 9	Comprehension Levels		
	Good	**Fair**	**Poor**
	%	%	%
(a) Layout with totally justified setting	67	19	14
(b) Layout with ragged right setting	38	22	40
(c) Layout with ragged left setting	10	18	72

The conclusion must be that ragged setting should be avoided if comprehensibility is to be maintained.

The comprehension level—or lack thereof—of ragged left setting was similar to that for sans serif body type, yet paradoxically, many designers who would never use ragged left setting have no qualms about ordering considerable volumes of setting in sans serif type.

It would be interesting if a future researcher were to quantify the comprehensibility of sans serif type set ragged left, as is seen frequently in some magazines and on display advertising.

Widows, jumps, and bastard measure

Throughout the research, readers were asked to express opinions on minor typographical elements, such as whether *widows* (lines of type of less than full length at the head of a column) annoyed them; their reactions when asked to jump from one page to another to continue an article; whether they found extremely narrow or extremely wide measure body type easy to read; whether reversed body type was acceptable; and the value of cross headings.

The results were calculated, and are expressed below as percentages.

Current newspapers and magazines were used to exemplify the elements being discussed.

Body Type

- 38 percent of readers found body type set wider than sixty characters hard to read. A further 22 percent indicated they probably wouldn't read wide measure body type, even though they didn't find any difficulty reading it.

- 87 percent said they found extremely narrow measure, such as less than twenty characters hard to read.

- 78 percent indicated they found cross headings useful, particularly in long articles. None said they found cross headings unattractive or intrusive.

- None said they were offended by, or even were aware of, widows. Apparently only printers and editors are offended.

- Only 7 percent of readers said they found body matter set in capitals easy to read. Readers were shown text set in 9 point Univers over 13 picas to a depth of 20 centimeters or 8 inches. A central section 5 centimeters or 2 inches deep was set in capitals, and readers were asked to indicate if they found this section easy to read. An overwhelming 93 percent said no. They were then shown similar material set to the same dimensions in Corona light, a serif face. The results were identical. When similar material was presented entirely in Univers lowercase, 22 percent said they found it easy to read. With Corona lowercase, 100 percent said they found it easy to read.

Headlines

- 57 percent said they disliked "screamer" headlines, such as are used on the front pages of many afternoon newspapers, and in some large display advertisements. This is because they had to hold the newspaper or magazine further than usual from the eyes, to be able to read the type. The reason for the annoyance was the need to focus twice to read the entire content. Some people might say, however, that it still doesn't stop them from being read.

- Multi-deck headlines were generally disliked. 56 percent indicated they found headlines of more than four decks difficult to comprehend.

- 68 percent said they became bored with long, wordy headlines. The comment was made frequently that there seemed to be nothing left to read after the headline. This, admittedly, is subjective—but the warning is there.

Design

- 61 percent of readers said that jumps, where an article is contained on a later page, or on several later pages in successive jumps, were annoying.

- 66 percent said they disliked pages which had large headlines with two or three paragraphs of copy, followed by an exhortation to jump to a later page. This was particularly disliked when the article was found to be inconsequential, or merely a newspaper promotion stunt.

- 83 percent said they usually disobeyed jumps. This may not concern advertising people, but what if their advertisement is on a jump page? It will need to be brilliant to be read.

- 39 percent said that if they were convinced to jump to continue reading an article, they frequently discovered they had not returned to where they were originally reading.

- 67 percent said they preferred illustrations to carry a description, such as a caption. The practice of describing an illustration in an accompanying article was frequently criticized.

- 81 percent said they found special screening effects on illustrations, such as mezzo, circular line, horizontal line, to be annoying. Some said they thought the screens were a device intended to disguise a poor illustration, or a printer's mistake.

- 77 percent said articles in which body type jumped over an illustration or cut-off headline, contrary to the natural flow of reading, annoyed them. The natural expectation was that once a barrier such as an illustration or cut-off was reached, the article would be continued at the head of the next block of type.

The moral is clear: it's not difficult to annoy a reader, either by inclusion or omission. And the message is also clear—before the editor or designer inserts a typographical element, he or she should think hard about the effect it may have on the reader.

Examples of body text settings

The following four pages contain exactly the same material - presented in slightly different ways.

Pages 65 and 66 illustrate wrong ways to set out body text, while Page 67 and 68 contain information set out in a more readable fashion.

Glance at pages 65 and 66, and read the box at the bottom of these pages illustrating why they are laid out incorrectly. Then read pages 67 and 68.

The range of fonts available for use with your version of PageMaker relates directly to the printer you are using. Provided with PC PageMaker for all supported printers, including the LaserJet Series II, are Dutch and Swiss in a variety of sizes and styles. (These are Times and Helvetica, respectively—a serif and a sans serif typeface.)

PostScript printers, however, use their own independent fonts. The average PostScript printer includes eleven typefaces, accessible from within PageMaker, and from these eleven fonts alone, given a font size range anywhere between 4 and 127, a combination of over 11,000 different fonts is possible.

Extra fonts can be purchased for all machines (including PostScript) that will allow you much more flexibility. Virtually any font available on a PostScript printer (up to 36 point and larger) can be purchased for your LaserJet Series II or compatible, installed in your software, and downloaded to your printer. There is no need to live with Dutch and Swiss alone.

Macintosh PageMaker users will normally have access to all eleven PostScript typefaces as standard.

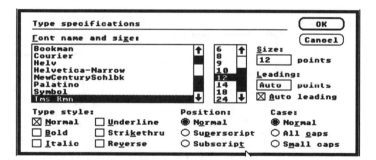

The above figure illustrates a range of fonts available to the PostScript PageMaker user.

Comments on this page:

The length of the line used on this page is too long. Readers struggle to read a line this wide, with poor legibility and comprehension the result. The width of these lines is about as wide as you would want to go (about sixty characters).

The range of fonts available for use with your version of PageMaker relates directly to the printer you are using. Provided with PC PageMaker for all supported printers, including the LaserJet Series II, are Dutch and Swiss in a variety of sizes and styles. (These are Times and Helvetica, respectively—a serif and a sans serif type face.)

PostScript printers, however, use their own independent fonts. The average PostScript printer includes eleven typefaces, accessible from within PageMaker, and from these eleven fonts alone, given a font size range anywhere between 4 and 127, a combination of over 11,000 different fonts is possible.

Extra fonts can be purchased for all machines (including PostScript) that will allow you much more flexibility. Virtually any font available on a PostScript printer (up to 36 point and larger) can be purchased for your LaserJet Series II or compatible, installed in your software, and downloaded to your printer. There is no need to live with Dutch and Swiss alone.

Macintosh PageMaker users will normally have access to all eleven PostScript typefaces as standard.

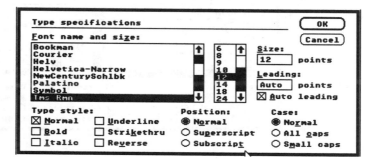

The above figure illustrates a range of fonts available to the PostScript PageMaker user.

Comments on this page:

The length of the line used on this page is good, but the typeface used is not. The research shows that Body Text in a sans serif typeface (in this case Helvetica) reduces comprehension by up to 50 percent.

The range of fonts available for use with your version of Page-Maker relates directly to the printer you are using. Provided with PC PageMaker for all supported printers, including the LaserJet Series II, are Dutch and Swiss in a variety of sizes and styles. (These are Times and Helvetica, respectively—a serif and a sans serif type face.)

PostScript printers, however, use their own independent fonts. The average PostScript printer includes eleven typefaces, accessible from within PageMaker, and from these eleven fonts alone, given a font size range anywhere between 4 and 127, a combination of over 11,000 different fonts is possible.

Extra fonts can be purchased for all machines (including Post-Script) that will allow you much more flexibility. Virtually any font available on a PostScript printer (up to 36 point and larger) can be purchased for your LaserJet Series II or compatible, installed in your software, and downloaded to your printer. There is no need to live with Dutch and Swiss alone.

Macintosh PageMaker users will normally have access to all eleven PostScript typefaces as standard.

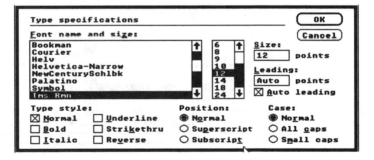

The above figure illustrates a range of fonts available to the PostScript PageMaker user.

Comments on this page:

> The length of the line used on this page is satisfactory. Also text is set in a serif type face (Palatino) and is a very readable 11 point on 13 point leading.

The range of fonts available for use with your version of PageMaker relates directly to the printer you are using. Provided with PC PageMaker for all supported printers, including the LaserJet Series II, are Dutch and Swiss in a variety of sizes and styles. (These are Times and Helvetica, respectively—a serif and a sans serif type face.)

PostScript printers, however, use their own independent fonts. The average PostScript printer includes eleven typefaces, accessible from within PageMaker, and from these eleven fonts alone, given a font size range anywhere between 4 and 127, a combination of over 11,000 different fonts is possible.

Extra fonts can be purchased for all machines (including PostScript) that will allow you much more flexibility. Virtually any font available on a PostScript printer (up to 36 point and larger) can be purchased for your LaserJet Series II or compatible, installed in your software, and downloaded to your printer. There is no need to live with Dutch and Swiss alone.

Macintosh PageMaker users will normally have access to all eleven PostScript typefaces as standard.

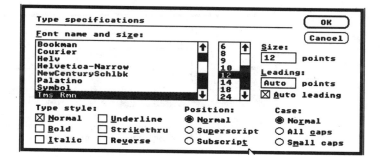

The above figure illustrates a range of fonts available to the PostScript PageMaker user.

Comments on this page:

The length of the line used on this page is satisfactory. Also text is set in a serif typeface (Times), and is a very readable 11 point on 13 point leading.

PageMaker font capabilities and options

With PageMaker installed on your PC or Macintosh, you initially have a limited number of fonts available for use. These fonts will vary depending upon your printer type. With the Hewlett-Packard LaserJet Series II, PC PageMaker initially comes bundled with the Bitstream Fontware package containing Dutch, Swiss, and Courier typefaces. Dutch and Swiss are similar to Times and Helvetica respectively. These fonts are downloaded to the printer from the computer as needed.

Other Bitstream fonts may be purchased to significantly enhance the number of typefaces available to the HP LaserJet Series II user.

For PageMaker Macintosh, and those PC PageMaker users that have PostScript printers, PageMaker uses the fonts that are contained within the printer—no initial downloading is required. For the original Apple LaserWriter, and Texas Instruments 2108 and 2115, this includes Courier, Helvetica, Times, and Symbol.

For other enhanced PostScript printers, such as the LaserWriter Plus, LaserWriter II NT, LaserWriter II NTX, NEC LC 890, AST TurboLaser/PS, Texas Instruments 2106 and QMS-PS 810, the Courier, Helvetica, Times, and Symbol are augmented by Helvetica Condensed, Palatino, Avant Garde, Bookman, Zapf Chancery, Zapf Dingbats, and New Century Schoolbook.

With PostScript capability, many of the included fonts can be used in normal, italic, bold, and bold italic modes, as well as in a wide variety of point sizes.

We will now look further into the font situation and see what other font capabilities may be incorporated within PageMaker.

Adobe fonts

Adobe is the company that produces the PostScript interpreter found in all laser printers and typesetters. As mentioned above, for PostScript printers, a number of fonts are already built into whatever PostScript printer you may be using.

Enhanced PostScript printers include the following font families shown below in 11 point size. Within PageMaker, these fonts can be chosen through the *Type* dialog box in any integer size between 4 and 127 points.

Helvetica
Normal
Oblique
Bold
Bold Oblique

Times Roman
Normal
Italic
Bold
Bold Italic

Courier
Normal
Oblique
Bold
Bold Oblique

Palatino
Normal
Italic
Bold
Bold Italic

New Century Schoolbook
Normal
Italic
Bold
Bold Italic

ITC Zapf Chancery Medium Italic

●✳✳✪✶❧✿✿
(ITC Zapf Dingbats)

ITC Bookman Light
Normal
Light Italic
Demi
Demi Italic

ITC Avant Garde Gothic Book
Normal
Gothic Book Oblique
Gothic Demi
Gothic Demi Oblique

Helvetica Condensed
Normal
Oblique
Bold
Bold Oblique

Σψμβολσ
(Symbol)

You can also purchase additional downloadable printer fonts to expand on what is available in the enhanced PostScript printers. Adobe offers a range of additional typeface families which can be loaded into a PostScript printer. Some of the additional Adobe fonts available include:

Optima, ITC Souvenir, ITC Lubalin Graph, ITC Garamond, ITC American Type/ITC Machine, ITC Benguiat/ITC Friz Quadrata, Glypha, Trump Mediaeval, Melior, ITC Galliard, ITC New Baskerville, ITC Korinna, Goudy Old Style, Sonata, Century Old Style, ITC Franklin Gothic, ITC Cheltenham, Park Avenue, Bodoni, Letter Gothic, Prestige Elite, Orator, News Gothic, ITC Tiffany, Cooper Black, Stencil/Hobo/Bushscript, Aachen/Revue/University Roman/Freestyle, and Carta.

Bitstream

Bitstream identifies itself as a digital type foundry company. It currently supplies digital type and related software to over 200 equipment manufacturers and software developers.

Bitstream offers its new concept of type called Fontware. This product can produce type fonts in any size from 6 points to 99.9 points, and can work with a range of screens and printers. It offers an alternative to the Adobe downloadable fonts and, more importantly, also offers desktop publishers an alternative to utilizing PostScript printers.

Why is this possible? Because PostScript, as part of its overall capabilities, allows any resident or downloadable font to be scaled in size over a very wide range of possibilities. For example, the Times typeface installed in the printer can be selected by Page-Maker in any point size from 4 to 127 points. This font flexibility is probably the major selling point of PostScript.

Fontware, by offering similar font scaling flexibility, now makes HP LaserJet type printers more attractive to a wider range of desktop publishing users.

Fontware comes in two different packages. First, there is the Fontware Installation Kit, and then there is a range of, currently, over 200 professional quality typefaces in a variety of weights and styles. The Installation Kit is used to customize each user's font library. A user would buy this Installation Kit and one or more Typeface Library packages based upon his/her requirements.

When users install Fontware on the PC for their desktop publishing program, they tell the program what screen display and printer they are using, and which typefaces, type sizes and character sets they would like. (They must have a typeface package for each typeface they would like to use.) They can create any type size their device can produce (from 6 to 99.9) points, and choose from a wide variety of character sets such as ASCII, Windows/ANSI, IBM PC, and HP Roman 8.

Based on their answers, Fontware will create the appropriate set of fonts for their screen and printer. These fonts are stored on the hard disk for future use at any time. Once created, the fonts will automatically appear in the menu of their desktop publishing program. There's no need to use Fontware again until they want to create new sizes, more fonts from new typeface packages, or new fonts for new devices.

Fontware includes both screen and printer fonts. Screens supported include EGA, Hercules, Wyse WY-700, Sigma Designs LaserView, and Moniterm Viking 1. Laser printer support includes HP LaserJet Plus, Series II and compatible, as well as PostScript printers.

In the Macintosh environment, fonts are installed through the Font/DA mover utility. The process is much easier as all Macintosh monitors are of the same high-resolution standard. Insert the font disk into your floppy drive. Double-click on the Font/DA utility (which should be resident in the system folder) and when on screen, click on Open. Select the fonts on the floppy disk and click Install. The fonts will download to your hard disk and will be there for your selection in PageMaker.

The top twenty Bitstream Fontware typefaces include:

1. Courier (10 pitch)
   - Courier Italic
   - Courier Bold
   - Courier Bold Italic

2. Prestige (12 pitch)
   - Prestige Italic
   - Prestige Bold
   - Prestige Bold Italic

3. Letter Gothic (12 pitch)
   - Letter Gothic Italic
   - Letter Gothic Bold
   - Letter Gothic Bold Italic

4. Swiss — Bitstream version of the Helvetica typeface
   - Swiss Italic
   - Swiss Bold
   - Swiss Bold Italic

5. Swiss Condensed
    Swiss Condensed Italic
    Swiss Condensed Bold
    Swiss Condensed Bold Italic

    Bitstream version of
    Helvetica Condensed
    typeface

6. Swiss Light
    Swiss Light Italic
    Swiss Black
    Swiss Black Italic

    Bitstream version of
    Helvetica Light
    typeface

7. Dutch
    Dutch Italic
    Dutch Bold
    Dutch Bold Italic

    Bitstream version of
    Times-Roman typeface

8. Zapf Calligraphic
    Zapf Calligraphic Italic
    Zapf Calligraphic Bold
    Zapf Calligraphic Bold Italics

    Bitstream version of
    Palatino typeface

9. Zapf Humanist
    Zapf Humanist Italic
    Zapf Humanist Bold
    Zapf Humanist Bold Italic

    Bitstream version of
    Optima typeface

10.Century Schoolbook
    Century Schoolbook Italic
    Century Schoolbook Bold
    Century Schoolbook Bold Italic

11. ITC Souvenir Light
    ITC Souvenir Light Italic
    ITC Souvenir Demi
    ITC Souvenir Demi Italic

12. ITC Garamond Book
> ITC Garamond Book Italic
> ITC Garamond Bold
> ITC Garamond Bold Italic

13. ITC Avant Garde Gothic Book
> ITC Avant Garde Gothic Medium
> ITC Avant Garde Gothic Demi
> ITC Avant Garde Gothic Bold

14. ITC Galliard
> ITC Galliard Italic
> ITC Galliard Bold
> ITC Galliard Bold Italic

15. ITC Korinna Regular
> ITC Korinna Kursiv Regular
> ITC Korinna Extra Bold
> ITC Korinna Kursiv Extra Bold

16. Bitstream Charter
> Bitstream Charter Italic
> Bitstream Charter Bold
> Bitstream Charter Bold Italic

17. Bitstream Cooper Black
> University Roman
> Cloister Black
> Broadway

18. Futura Book
> Futura Book Italic
> Futura Heavy
> Futura Heavy Italic

19. Futura Medium
    Futura Medium Italic
    Futura Bold
    Futura Bold Italic

20. Futura Light
    Futura Light Italic
    Futura Medium Condensed
    Futura Extra Black

Typeface examples

On the next ten pages are examples of various typefaces using normal, italic, bold, and bold italic variants.

Helvetica

10 Point Examples of Helvetica

No rekeying of text is required, as page makeup packages can accept text directly from many standard word processing files. The powerful page layout capabilities that are generally available allow for text to be accurately positioned on each page in a multi-column format, as well as the required headings, subheadings, page numbers, etc. Text height and font can be easily modified, and different column variations can be quickly achieved.

No rekeying of text is required, as page makeup packages can accept text directly from many standard word processing files. The powerful page layout capabilities that are generally available allow for text to be accurately positioned on each page in a multi-column format, as well as the required headings, subheadings, page numbers, etc. Text height and font can be easily modified, and different column variations can be quickly achieved.

No rekeying of text is required, as page makeup packages can accept text directly from many standard word processing files. The powerful page layout capabilities that are generally available allow for text to be accurately positioned on each page in a multi-column format, as well as the required headings, subheadings, page numbers, etc. Text height and font can be easily modified, and different column variations can be quickly achieved.

No rekeying of text is required, as page makeup packages can accept text directly from many standard word processing files. The powerful page layout capabilities that are generally available allow for text to be accurately positioned on each page in a multi-column format, as well as the required headings, subheadings, page numbers, etc. Text height and font can be easily modified, and different column variations can be quickly achieved.

Times

10 Point Examples of Times

No rekeying of text is required, as page makeup packages can accept text directly from many standard word processing files. The powerful page layout capabilities that are generally available allow for text to be accurately positioned on each page in a multi-column format, as well as the required headings, subheadings, page numbers, etc. Text height and font can be easily modified and different column variations can be quickly achieved.

No rekeying of text is required, as page makeup packages can accept text directly from many standard word processing files. The powerful page layout capabilities that are generally available allow for text to be accurately positioned on each page in a multi-column format, as well as the required headings, subheadings, page numbers, etc. Text height and font can be easily modified, and different column variations can be quickly achieved.

No rekeying of text is required, as page makeup packages can accept text directly from many standard word processing files. The powerful page layout capabilities that are generally available allow for text to be accurately positioned on each page in a multi-column format, as well as the required headings, subheadings, page numbers, etc. Text height and font can be easily modified and different column variations can be quickly achieved.

No rekeying of text is required, as page makeup packages can accept text directly from many standard word processing files. The powerful page layout capabilities that are generally available allow for text to be accurately positioned on each page in a multi-column format, as well as the required headings, subheadings, page numbers, etc. Text height and font can be easily modified, and different column variations can be quickly achieved.

Courier

10 Point Examples of Courier

No rekeying of text is required, as page makeup packages can accept text directly from many standard word processing files. The powerful page layout capabilities that are generally available allow for text to be accurately positioned on each page in a multi-column format, as well as the required headings, subheadings, page numbers, etc. Text height and font can be easily modified, and different column variations can be quickly achieved.

No rekeying of text is required, as page makeup packages can accept text directly from many standard word processing files. The powerful page layout capabilities that are generally available allow for text to be accurately positioned on each page in a multi-column format, as well as the required headings, subheadings, page numbers, etc. Text height and font can be easily modified, and different column variations can be quickly achieved.

No rekeying of text is required, as page makeup packages can accept text directly from many standard word processing files. The powerful page layout capabilities that are generally available allow for text to be accurately positioned on each page in a multi-column format, as well as the required headings, subheadings, page numbers, etc. Text height and font can be easily modified, and different column variations can be quickly achieved.

No rekeying of text is required, as page makeup packages can accept text directly from many standard word processing files. The powerful page layout capabilities that are generally available allow for text to be accurately positioned on each page in a multi-column format, as well as the required headings, subheadings, page numbers, etc. Text height and font can be easily modified, and different column variations can be quickly achieved

Avant-Garde

10 Point Examples of Avant-Garde

No rekeying of text is required, as page makeup packages can accept text directly from many standard word processing files. The powerful page layout capabilities that are generally available allow for text to be accurately positioned on each page in a multi-column format, as well as the required headings, subheadings, page numbers, etc. Text height and font can be easily modified, and different column variations can be quickly achieved.

No rekeying of text is required, as page makeup packages can accept text directly from many standard word processing files. The powerful page layout capabilities that are generally available allow for text to be accurately positioned on each page in a multi-column format, as well as the required headings, subheadings, page numbers, etc. Text height and font can be easily modified, and different column variations can be quickly achieved.

No rekeying of text is required, as page makeup packages can accept text directly from many standard word processing files. The powerful page layout capabilities that are generally available allow for text to be accurately positioned on each page in a multi-column format, as well as the required headings, subheadings, page numbers, etc. Text height and font can be easily modified, and different column variations can be quickly achieved.

No rekeying of text is required, as page makeup packages can accept text directly from many standard word processing files. The powerful page layout capabilities that are generally available allow for text to be accurately positioned on each page in a multi-column format, as well as the required headings, subheadings, page numbers, etc. Text height and font can be easily modified, and different column variations can be quickly achieved.

Bookman

10 Point Examples of Bookman

No rekeying of text is required, as page makeup packages can accept text directly from many standard word processing files. The powerful page layout capabilities that are generally available allow for text to be accurately positioned on each page in a multi-column format, as well as the required headings, subheadings, page numbers, etc. Text height and font can be easily modified, and different column variations can be quickly achieved.

No rekeying of text is required, as page makeup packages can accept text directly from many standard word processing files. The powerful page layout capabilities that are generally available allow for text to be accurately positioned on each page in a multi-column format, as well as the required headings, subheadings, page numbers, etc. Text height and font can be easily modified, and different column variations can be quickly achieved.

No rekeying of text is required, as page makeup packages can accept text directly from many standard word processing files. The powerful page layout capabilities that are generally available allow for text to be accurately positioned on each page in a multi-column format, as well as the required headings, subheadings, page numbers, etc. Text height and font can be easily modified, and different column variations can be quickly achieved.

No rekeying of text is required, as page makeup packages can accept text directly from many standard word processing files. The powerful page layout capabilities that are generally available allow for text to be accurately positioned on each page in a multi-column format, as well as the required headings, subheadings, page numbers, etc. Text height and font can be easily modified, and different column variations can be quickly achieved.

Helvetica Narrow

10 Point Examples of Helvetica Narrow

No rekeying of text is required as page makeup packages can accept text directly from many standard word processing files. The powerful page layout capabilities that are generally available allow for text to be accurately positioned on each page in a multi-column format, as well as the required headings, sub-headings page numbers etc. Text height and font can be easily modified and different column variations can be quickly achieved.

No rekeying of text is required as page makeup packages can accept text directly from many standard word processing files. The powerful page layout capabilities that are generally available allow for text to be accurately positioned on each page in a multi-column format, as well as the required headings, sub-headings page numbers etc. Text height and font can be easily modified and different column variations can be quickly achieved.

No rekeying of text is required as page makeup packages can accept text directly from many standard word processing files. The powerful page layout capabilities that are generally available allow for text to be accurately positioned on each page in a multi-column format, as well as the required headings, sub-headings page numbers etc. Text height and font can be easily modified and different column variations can be quickly achieved.

No rekeying of text is required as page makeup packages can accept text directly from many standard word processing files. The powerful page layout capabilities that are generally available allow for text to be accurately positioned on each page in a multi-column format, as well as the required headings, sub-headings page numbers etc. Text height and font can be easily modified and different column variations can be quickly achieved.

Palatino

10 Point Examples of Palatino

No rekeying of text is required, as page makeup packages can accept text directly from many standard word processing files. The powerful page layout capabilities that are generally available allow for text to be accurately positioned on each page in a multi-column format, as well as the required headings, subheadings, page number,s etc. Text height and font can be easily modified, and different column variations can be quickly achieved.

No rekeying of text is required, as page makeup packages can accept text directly from many standard word processing files. The powerful page layout capabilities that are generally available allow for text to be accurately positioned on each page in a multi-column format, as well as the required headings, subheadings, page numbers, etc. Text height and font can be easily modified, and different column variations can be quickly achieved.

No rekeying of text is required, as page makeup packages can accept text directly from many standard word processing files. The powerful page layout capabilities that are generally available allow for text to be accurately positioned on each page in a multi-column format, as well as the required headings, subheadings, page numbers, etc. Text height and font can be easily modified and different column variations can be quickly achieved.

No rekeying of text is required, as page makeup packages can accept text directly from many standard word processing files. The powerful page layout capabilities that are generally available allow for text to be accurately positioned on each page in a multi-column format, as well as the required headings, subheadings, page numbers, etc. Text height and font can be easily modified, and different column variations can be quickly achieved.

Century Schoolbook

10 Point Examples of Century Schoolbook

No rekeying of text is required as page makeup packages can accept text directly from many standard word processing files. The powerful page layout capabilities that are generally available allow for text to be accurately positioned on each page in a multi-column format, as well as the required headings, subheadings, page numbers, etc. Text height and font can be easily modified, and different column variations can be quickly achieved.

No rekeying of text is required, as page makeup packages can accept text directly from many standard word processing files. The powerful page layout capabilities that are generally available allow for text to be accurately positioned on each page in a multi-column format, as well as the required headings, subheadings, page numbers, etc. Text height and font can be easily modified, and different column variations can be quickly achieved.

No rekeying of text is required, as page makeup packages can accept text directly from many standard word processing files. The powerful page layout capabilities that are generally available allow for text to be accurately positioned on each page in a multi-column format, as well as the required headings, subheadings, page numbers, etc. Text height and font can be easily modified, and different column variations can be quickly achieved.

No rekeying of text is required, as page makeup packages can accept text directly from many standard word processing files. The powerful page layout capabilities that are generally available allow for text to be accurately positioned on each page in a multi-column format, as well as the required headings, subheadings, page numbers, etc. Text height and font can be easily modified, and different column variations can be quickly achieved.

Zapf Chancery

10 Point Example of Zapf Chancery

No rekeying of text is required, as page makeup packages can accept text directly from many standard word processing files. The powerful page layout capabilities that are generally available allow for text to be accurately positioned on each page in a multi-column format, as well as the required headings, subheadings, page numbers, etc. Text height and font can be easily modified, and different column variations can be quickly achieved.

Zapf Dingbats (❖❋■✳❂❀▼▲)

10 Point Example of Zapf Dingbats

★❑ ❑❋❋❅❋❋■❋ ❑❂ ▼❂❋▼ ❋▲ ❑❋❑◆❋❋❑❋❋✵ ❂▲ ❑❂❋❋ ❀❂❋❋◆❑
❑❂❋❋❂❋❋▲ ❋❂■ ❂❋❋❋❑▼ ▼❂❋▼ ❋❋❑❋❋▼❀❍ ❂❑❑❀ ❀❑❂■
▲▼❂■❂❑❂ ❑❑❑❋ ❑❑❑❋❋▲▲❋■❋ ❋❋❂●▲▲ ❋❋❋ ❑❑❋❑❋◆●
❑❑❋❋ ❀❑❑◆▼ ❋❂❑❑❀❂❂▼❂▼▲ ▼❋❂▼ ❂❑❋ ❋❋■❋❑❀❀❑
❀❋❀❋❀❀❀❑ ❀❀❑❑❐ ❀❑❑ ▼❂❍▼ ▼❑ ❀❋ ❀❋❋◆❀❑❀▼❋❀❍ ❑❑▲❋❋
▼❋❑■❋❋ ❑■ ❋❀❋❋ ❑❀❋❋ ❋■ ❀ ❀◆❀▼❋❋■❋❀◆❀❑■ ❋❑❑❀❀▼✵
❀▲ ❐❋●● ❀▲ ▼❋❋ ❑❀❑◆❋❑❑❋❋ ❋❋❀❋■❋▲❂✵ ▲❂◆❋❀❀❋■❋▲
❑❀❋❋ ■◆❀❀❋❑▲✵ ❋▼❋❂❍ ❋❋❍▼ ❋❋❋❋▼▼ ❀■❋ ❀❑■▼ ❋❀■ ❀❋
❋❀▲❂❋❍ ❑❑❋❋❋❋❋❋✵ ❀■❋ ❋❋❋❋❋❑■▼ ❋❑●◆❑■ ◆❑❑❋❂☞
▼❋❑■▲ ❋❀■ ❀❋ ❑❀◆❋❋❀❍ ❀❋❋❋❋◆❋❋☞

Chapter 5
Guidelines For Newsletters

Chapter 5
Guidelines For Newsletters

Newsletters are common methods of communication. They are used to communicate within organizations (as staff newsletters) or to communicate with the outside world (customer newsletters).

Based on the theories already discussed throughout this book, some of the major points to consider when putting together a newsletter are elaborated on below.

Let's consider the first page of, say, a four-page newsletter. Important considerations here include (some of which were discussed in Chapter 4):

- Don't overdo the Masthead (the newsletter name) or the various story headlines. Within the research undertaken, 57 percent of respondents said they disliked "screamer" headlines. Sixty-eight percent became bored with long wordy headlines.

- Headlines can be serif or sans serif. Studies showed very little difference for readers in this regard.

- Don't try to crowd the first page with lots of stories which are all continued on subsequent pages, 61 percent of readers say that these jumps are annoying. Eighty-three percent said they usually disobeyed jumps.

- Make sure the headlines are in both upper and lowercase.

Apart from the first page, the following major points should be carefully considered:

- Keep the body text size appropriate to the audience—at least 10 to 12 point, no smaller.

- Include a reasonable amount of graphics and captions. Another important research finding was that 67 percent preferred illustrations to carry a caption. Seventy-seven percent said articles in which body type jumped over an illustration were annoying.

- Use italics for captions—normally at one point size smaller than the body type.

- All body text should be serif, not sans serif type. (Refer back to Chapter 4, where studies showed reader comprehension levels were 67 percent versus 12 percent on serif versus sans serif type.)

- Use at least two columns per page, and preferably three.

- Unequal column widths can add variety. For example, if using three-column format, on one page it would be good to run text across two columns. Such stories can often be boxed.

- Headers and footers are useful to define such things as page number, newsletter name, and newsletter date.

- Double-sided printing is more professional than single-sided.

- Consider use of vertical rules between columns. There is no correct yes or no on this, it depends on overall page design.

- Special symbols should be used to end stories. This reduces any confusion where multiple stories are contained on one page.

- Don't put barriers in the way of body text, particularly if the story continues down the page. Research has shown that once a barrier is reached, the article is expected to continue at the head of the next block or column.

Good and bad examples

Let's look at some newsletter examples:

Figures 1 to 4 indicate badly designed first pages for the reasons as discussed in the captions. Figures 5 and 6 are acceptable front pages. Other suitable designs are also possible. For example, the exercise we performed in Chapter 3.

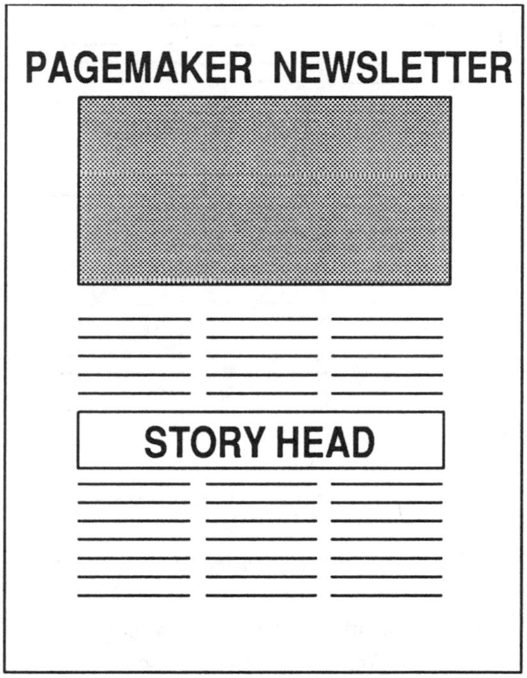

PAGEMAKER NEWSLETTER

STORY HEAD

Figure 1.
This is not acceptable for the following reasons:

(i) Long headlines are not satisfactory if all in uppercase. This headline is probably OK.
(ii) No caption on the picture.
(iii) Story headline is set in the middle of the text.

Figure 2.
This is not attractive for the following reasons:

(i) Uppercase headlines too long.
(ii) Picture has no caption.
(iii) Picture breaks up body text in the middle of the page. Some readers would move up to the top of the third column after reaching the picture at the middle of column two.

Figure 3.
This is not attractive for the following reasons:

(i) Uppercase headlines too long.
(ii) Masthead is kerned too tightly.
(iii) Too many "Continued on page x." This is annoying to many readers.
(iv) Picture has no caption.

Figure 4.
This is not attractive for the following reasons:

(i) Uppercase headlines too long.
(ii) Picture has no caption.
(iii) Text is set ragged right, not justified. Research has shown that justified versus ragged right has a 67 percent versus 38 percent comprehension advantage.
(iv) Picture breaks up body text in the middle of the page. See further comments in point (iii) of Figure 2.

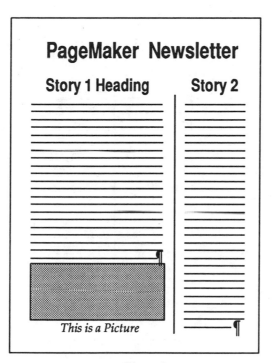

Figure 5.
This is an acceptable front page for a number of reasons, including:

(i) Masthead is not too large or long to overpower the rest of the page.
(ii) Body text is set justified, 11 point, serif type.
(iii) Picture does not break up the body text and includes a caption.
(iv) No "Continued on page x" stories.
(v) Story headings are upper and lowercase.
(vi) Unequal columns add variety and interest to the front page.
(vii) Masthead and story headings are black text on white background.
(viii) Stories 1 and 2 have end-of-story symbols.
(ix) Body text is uses 11 point on 13 point line spacing.

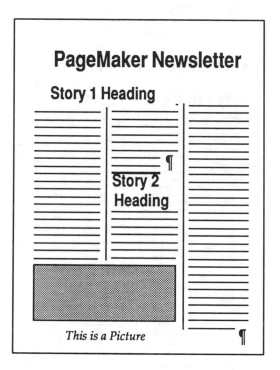

Figure 6.
This is an acceptable front page for a number of reasons, including:

(i) Masthead is not too large or long to overpower the rest of the page.
(ii) Body text is set justified, 11 point, serif type.
(iii) Picture does not break up the body text and includes a caption.
(iv) No "Continued on page x" stories.
(v) Story headings are upper and lowercase.
(vi) Three columns are attractive.
(vii) Masthead and story headings are black text on white background.
(viii) Stories 1 and 2 have end-of-story symbols.
(ix) Body text is 11 point on 13 point line spacing.

Chapter 5 Exercise

Newsletters: The Inside Pages

This exercise is designed to outline the basic standards discussed so far in creating a newsletter master, that can be used on a repetitive basis. It is a continuation of the Chapter 3 Exercise—Getting Started.

To begin, open the document "Newsletter" created earlier. Open the original template and not an untitled copy, so that changes we now make can be stored in the template.

We now wish to set up the specifications for pages 2, 3, and 4. First, we will apply the headers and footers to the Master pages.

- Go to the Left master page and create two horizontal, 4-point lines as follows: The first line is positioned 1/4 inch above the top margin, and the second line positioned 1/4 inch below the bottom margin. When this is done, copy and paste on the right master page.

- Create a paragraph style for the header. The attributes should be 10 point Times (Dutch), Italic, all paragraph indentations to be set at 0, clear all tabs and set a right tab at the far right margin (at 6.5 inches).

- At the top of the left master page create the page number at left) and date (at right). (For PageMaker on the Mac type in "Page" space, then, holding down the Option and Command keys, type "P" to apply automatic page numbering. For PageMaker on the PC, the key sequence is Ctrl-Shift-3.) Tab across and type in the word "Date" at the right-hand tab.

- Apply the header paragraph style to the page number and date line. Now position this information above the top left horizontal line. For the right master page, reverse the typing sequence so the pages will show a mirror image (i.e., Date, tab, then Page Number), and apply the same paragraph style.

- The footer can be applied with the header paragraph style as it has the same attributes. It will be positioned at the bottom of the left and right page as shown in Figure 7. We

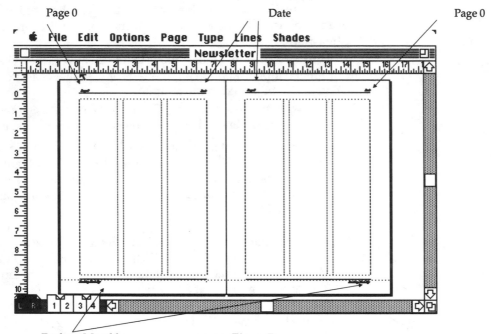

Figure 7.

The Master pages setup. Your pages should look similar to this.

want to identify the Newsletter, so type in "Desktop Monthly" as our footer. Apply the Header paragraph style. Your result should look similar to Figure 7 below.

- The headers and footers are now set to appear on each page of the newsletter. (To prevent the master items appearing on any page, go to that page and deselect the *Display Master Items* command in the **Page** menu.)

- The basic layout for the inside pages is complete. Note that you can have as many inside pages as required. However, we will assume a four page newsletter for our example.

- The final page will be set up similar to Figure 8 below. The header is included, as for pages 2 and 3, although the footer is not there. At the bottom of the page we have included details on company information. The steps to set this up are explained below.

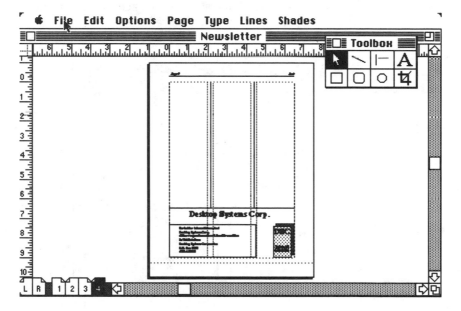

Figure 8.
The final page will look similar to this.

- There are two ways to present the header without the footer. Either create an invisible box over the footer (which we have done), or deselect *Display master items* in the **Page** menu and recreate the header information separately.

- Create a rectangle with a 2-point thickness to house the company information. The size will be variable, depending on the amount of information it will contain. We have included a company logo to the right of the box. See Figure 9 for these details.

- Insert a horizontal line above these two items, allowing enough space below this line to include the company name.

- For this exercise we created a dummy address and included a simple logo. You may like to experiment with this yourself to see what kind of result you can achieve. The result of our example is displayed in Figure 9.

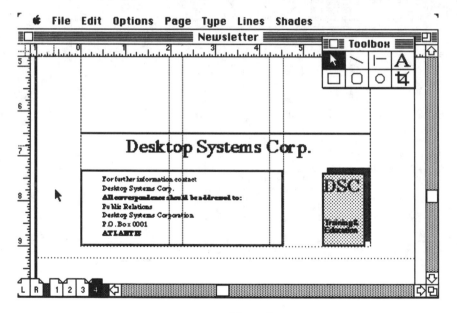

Figure 9.
The company information, once typed in, can look like this on completion.

- Save your template now, as we will be using this as the master document in the Chapter 8 exercise. We will then create a full newsletter complete with text and graphics.

Chapter 6
Understanding Proportion

Chapter 6
Understanding Proportion

Excellent design concepts can be turned into practical failures if the page proportions are not balanced.

There are a number of schools of thought on what is the most appropriate proportion for a printed page, but each school agrees on one point—the most agreeable shape is oblong.

The two basic shapes are: *regular oblong*, the proportions of which are two to three; or *Golden oblong*, the proportions of which are three to five.

A4 and Letter page size are approximately regular oblong, with A4 being the closer of the two. Foolscap is Golden oblong. Any of these pages are generally accepted as a good design shape. The oblong can be placed either vertically (portrait), or horizontally (landscape).

Portrait is generally the more popular for most publications. A research study conducted in Germany showed that 80% of readers will go to a vertical design in preference to a horizontal one.

The other common sense point in reference to proportion is to always consider the destination of the design. Don't make a leaflet 9 inches long if it has to fit into an envelope 8.8 inches long.

Type units

There are two basic forms of design; *traditional* and *modern*. Traditional is symmetrical and passive, while modern is generally asymmetrical and active.

The traditional method of dividing the depth of the page up into eight equal parts is very effective. The third division from the top is what the Greeks called *the line of golden proportion*—and it is considered the best position for one group of words or a single word (i.e., front page of a report). (See Figure 1 on the next page.)

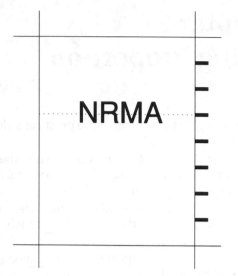

Figure 1.
The line of golden proportion.

Shape and type harmony

When type is placed on a piece of paper, it should harmonize with the piece of paper. The shape of the type should harmonize with the shape of the paper.

A wide group of type on a long narrow sheet of paper isn't pleasing to the reader's eye because there is no relationship between the type and the page. If the type group is too wide for the page it looks unbalanced.

It is not necessary to change type styles to achieve a good display. Sufficient contrast can be achieved by using a variety of types within one family. When one style is used, type harmony is guaranteed.

When a blend of types is desired to create a layout, great care should be taken that the styles are compatible.

Geometric sans serif and most Roman types blend well, as do Roman and Italic type. Roman and Script are generally compatible. While script and italic have similar characteristics, they should not be used together.

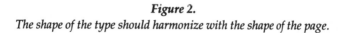

Figure 2.
The shape of the type should harmonize with the shape of the page.

Chapter 7
Tone Harmony and Contrast

Chapter 7
Tone Harmony and Contrast

Creating type that "talks"

Tone harmony on the printed page is achieved when the various elements—type, borders, illustrations, and rules—have an even, uniform tone.

When the tone is uniform, all elements blend into an even gray or black—a fundamental requirement.

There are also times when contrast is needed, but to achieve contrast a designer must first understand harmony.

Types used for text are usually designed to present an even gray tone—and if other elements are to become part of the page they should be selected to harmonize with the type. If any of these elements were to have a darker tone they would cause the printed page to appear spotty.

Dark spots are permissible if contrast is desired. Without thought, achieving contrast in this manner may sacrifice an important part of the message.

Dark spots draw the eye like a magnet—possibly causing them to miss important material. They also have the effect of creating a halo around themselves, making the surrounding type difficult to read.

This applies particularly to large drop caps, border decorations and fancy rules or graphics work. An ornament that is too heavy may stand out from the page to the detriment of some of the surrounding text. This will violate one of the cardinal rules—that design should be invisible.

For example, a design with illustrations that are bold in tone should be accompanied by slightly bold type.

See the examples on the following two pages showing tone harmony and lack of tone harmony.

"Invoices paid within 48 hours? Are you pulling my leg?"

Imagine clients who pay in two days instead of sixty.

Imagine what you could do with that extra cash.

Far from being widly impossible, its remarkably easy with factoring from the Better Business Company.

Quite simply, we'll buy your outstanding invoices for cash less a small service fee.

There are no burdensome repayments.The problem of receiving the funds is our business.

We'll do this in consultation with you and your credit manager, by assigning a Better Business executive to your business. We'll also provide information to help you in your business: aged debtor lists, sales and territory analyses, and sound financial advice.

These are just a few of the factors that distinguish Better Business factoring. Call us for an appointment and we'll show you some more.

Better Business Company Finance & Service Division

Figure 1
This page lacks tone harmony—or harmony of any kind.

Invoices paid within 48hours

Are you pulling my leg...

Imagine clients who pay in two days instead of sixty. Imagine what you could do with that extra cash!

Far from being widly impossible, its remarkably easy with factoring from the Better Business Company.

Quite simply, we'll buy your outstanding invoices for cash less a small service fee.

There are no burdensome repayments.

The problem of receiving the funds is our business. We'll do this in consultation with you and your credit manager, by assigning a Better Business executive to your business. We'll also provide information to help you in your business: aged debtor lists, sales and territory analyses, and sound financial advice.

These are just a few of the factors that distinguish Better Business factoring.

Call us for an appointment and we'll show you some more.

Better Business Company
Finance & Service Division

Figure 2.
With heavy illustration, heavy headline, and heavy text type, this page has tone harmony.

Contrast

One of the design principles we should apply widely in putting punch into designs is *contrast*.

Contrast is the use of type, illustration, and other elements in such a way that prominence is given to certain features.

Contrast causes elements of a design to stand out, making them instantly and strikingly apparent. Punch can be applied to a printed piece through use of contrast.

A tall building among low ones, or a flash of light, compels attention by contrast with their surrounds, or with what the mind usually associates with normal conditions.

However, contrast is best if not handled as a sledgehammer in a china store.

There are other ways of achieving contrast than with black ink. Other ways include: changed type font for a key word, italic, slightly larger type, underscore, etc.

Contrast should make the type talk. It should make the person reading the message accent certain words.

Avoid the use, however, of too many display lines or groups, as well as the use of too many different sizes of type. It is more effective to emphasize only one or two words.

Talking with type is much like speaking before an audience. A speaker who adds force to a word or two is much more successful than one who screams at the audience. The same applies to design work.

Chapter 8
Balance

Chapter 8
Balance

Easy on the reader

Balance plays an important role in design, both vertical and horizontal. There are even two forms of vertical balance—*formal* and *informal*.

Formal design is symmetrical. If a line is drawn down the vertical center of the page, half the display units will be on one side and half on the other. This is appropriate for formal, but not for more dynamic informal designs. Formal balance would generally be used for more conservative designs, say insurance bonds, stock market reports, etc.

Informal balance would be used with more personal messages, i.e., newsletters, consumables, etc.

To achieve horizontal balance, the first step is to determine the optical center of the page. Because of an optical illusion, the real mathematical center of a page will strike the reader as being too low. For this reason, a line slightly above true center is used as the axis about which two outstanding units are balanced.

The optical center line is about one tenth of the distance between the actual center and the top of the page.

Imagine the optical center as a see-saw. if two boys of equal size are on the see-saw, sitting at points equally distant from the fulcrum, or optical center line, they will balance.

Therefore, if you had two illustrations of equal size or strength, they should be placed at equal distance from the optical center.

Now, if one of the boys on the see-saw was much larger and heavier than the other, he would have to sit closer to the fulcrum to balance the smaller boy.

Likewise, if we have groups of type or illustrations of unequal size, the larger unit should be placed nearer the optical center than the smaller one.

Strength, or blackness of type, should also be balanced. A color at the top must be balanced with some color in the lower half. Paradoxically this need not be of the same strength as the color in the top half to gain an optical balance.

See examples of balance in the diagrams below and on the following pages.

Figure 1.
Formal balance.

Figure 2.
Informal balance.

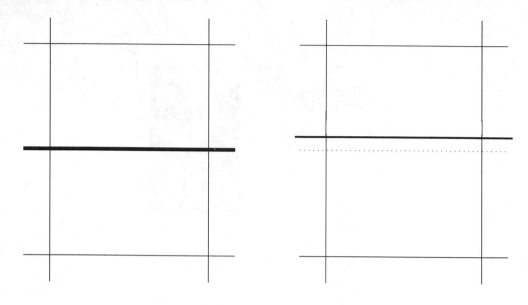

Figure 3.
Geometrical center.

Figure 4.
Optical center.

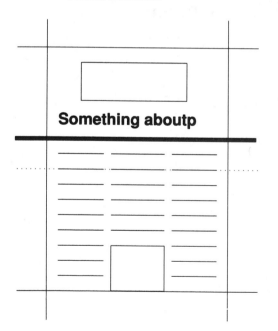

Figure 5.
Fat boy and thin boy.

Chapter 8 Exercise

Newsletters: Balance

In this exercise we are going to use the template Newsletter created in the Chapter 5 exercise. We need to open it as an untitled publication, and lay out text and graphics from the Getting Started files. This exercise can be performed under PageMaker on either a Macintosh or a PC . As a guide, we have printed and included a copy of the newsletter (pages 126 to 129) you are going to create. Refer to these pages before starting, to get a feel for how the layout should look.

- Step one in this exercise is to open the template Newsletter.

- Upon opening you will notice it automatically copies the template and opens as an untitled version. If you wish, you could name the newsletter relevant to the publication; for example, December Issue. We have kept the title for this example as *Desktop Monthly*.

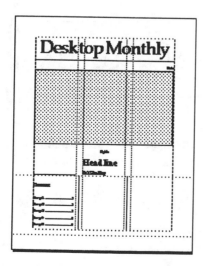

Figure 6.
Open the template Newsletter as a new,
untitled publication.

- Comfortable with the knowledge that the original template cannot be altered, we can now load the text and graphic files into this document for this month's newsletter.

- To experiment with this layout, and to get a feel for the techniques required, we are going to load in a number of PageMaker sample files from the Getting Started folder (Macintosh) or directory (PC). They include:
  Photo.tif
  Radius.eps
  Quadrille.eps
  BCover.eps
  Brochure.txt
  Bulletin.txt
  (Depending on which type of computer—PC or Macintosh—you are using, these names will be a little different.)

- Before loading these files, the date in the left and right header of the master pages should be changed to reflect the Newsletter. Also, the date on the first page can be altered through the normal text editing procedure. Figure 7 shows the dates on page 1, after performing these procedures.

Figure 7.
The first page reflecting the header and the new date once they have been changed.

- We are now ready to format all our newsletter items.

- First, load Photo.tif into the specified picture frame on the first page, adjusting its size to suit with the pointer tool. The gray background in the frame beneath the picture is purely for effect. You may add your own special touch if you choose. The caption "Our editor - hard at work!" was then included below the picture by deleting "caption" with the text cursor, and keying in this statement. In this way the caption paragraph style will be maintained.

Figure 8.

Starting to build the newsletter. At this stage we have changed the date, placed Photo.tif into the picture frame, and edited the caption paragraph.

- The next step is to place Brochure.txt.
  Having selected the Brochure file, choose *Autoflow* from the **Options** menu and hold the Shift key down as you place the text into column two. (Holding the Shift key will give you semi-auto flow control so you can lay one column at a time.)

- Selet and cut the actual heading "New Colors for the Home" from the main body of text, and insert it where the Headline paragraph is (see result on page 126). We have deleted the subheading on the newsletter altogether. This is the new story title.

Figure 9.
Cutting and Pasting the new Heading.

- Complete the layout of the text on page 2. The text should fit in the first two columns. For this exercise, we have altered this particular text block to the point where we have taken some of the original text out. In any newsletter or publication, copy fitting (mentioned in Chapter 3) quite often requires words and paragraphs to be edited so that the text fits into its allocated space.

- As you may very well discover, depending on the printer you have and whether you are using PageMaker on a Macintosh or on a PC or compatible, the text and graphics may not fit exactly the way they appear in these screen shots. The main points being emphasized in this exercise are to get the final result to look good by abiding by the principles put forward in this book. It may take a few attempts, but once the principles are understood, the results will show.

There are a number of ways to achieve successful copy fitting. You will need to utilize these methods to fit the text where required.

- Edit the text.

- Resize pictures or graphics on the page.

- Create new tags for subheadings of different sizes.

- Change font size and/or leading of main body of text.

- The next step in this exercise is to bring in the two image files Radius and Quadrille, and fit them in the top two columns of page 2 as illustrated in Figure 10 below, and page 127. A caption has been included below the two pictures.

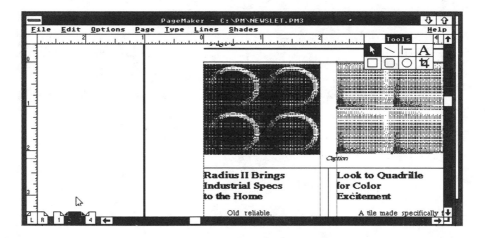

Figure 10.

The two image files Radius and Quadrille have been placed and positioned in the two columns on the left. Notice also that the two subheading paragraphs of the Brochure.Txt file have been applied the Subhead style.

- The next step is to bring in the Bulletin text file and begin placing it at the top of the third column of page 2. It will run over into the fourth page, but once you have brought in the final picture you can manipulate this text to fit your requirement.

- At this stage, bring in the large image file BCover and place it on the third page similar to that shown below in Figure 11 and page 128.

The Bulletin txt file begins here

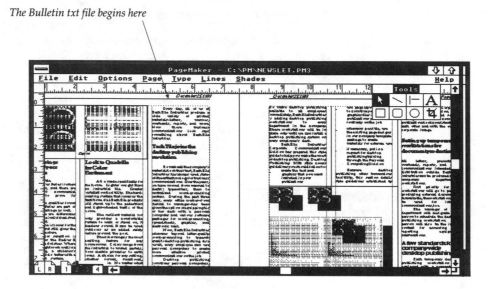

Figure 11.
Pages 2 and 3 once resizing the text and picture files.

- From here it is up to you to adjust the text so that it all fits, and abides by the basic principles of good typography. As a guideline these include :

  • Most text is justified (bullets and main points can be an exception if there are not too many).

  • Pictures do not break reading patterns.

  • Pictures have captions.

  • Subheadings do not overpower body text

- You will notice that the second story will have gone onto the fourth page and perhaps created a fifth page. Once you have fitted the text onto pages 2, 3, and 4, simply delete page 5.

- For the finishing touches we have added thin lines around the pictures and included vertical rules within the columns of text. The result of our effort producing this sample newsletter is contained on the following four pages.

That completes this exercise in layout and design.

The next four pages display the newsletter sample created in this exercise.

We have also included, at the end of this chapter, six pages extracted from PageMaker 3 by Example (M&T Books, 1989), to explain the benefits of text and graphic placeholders when doing repetitive brochures and newsletters. See pages 130 to 135 for these details.

Remember, the key to any design and layout is simplicity. Whenever your audience doesn't have to struggle with the article, they will remain interested.

Desktop Monthly

December 25th, 1988

Our editor - hard at work!

New Colors
for the Home

Contents

Story 1 1

Story 2 2

Story 3 3

Story 4 4

Story 5 5

We have always been the top floor where it counts: underfoot. In bank lobbies, in office reception areas, in hotel kitchens, in hospitals.

And now we have come home.

TechTile has studied the needs of the modern home and homeowner and designed a new line of studded rubber flooring for the noncommercial setting.

Many of the demands are the same. Rugged, scuff-proof surface, a full range of colors, finishes from high-gloss to semi-transparent. But the home setting has its own criteria: smaller patterns, softer edges, warmer colors.

TechTile for the home should be considered for the kitchen and the bathroom, for children's playrooms and bedrooms. It is as impervious to spills as it is to foot traffic. Upkeep is minimal. And it is quiet. You may find the patter of little feet reduced from a dull roar to a whisper.

Desktop Monthly

Caption

Every day, all of us at TechTile Industries produce a wide variety of printed materials—letters, memos, overheads, reports, and more. How those business communications look says something about TechTile Industries.

TechTile joins the desktop publishing revolution

To make all the company's materials look their best, TechTile Industries has always used state-of-the-art technology for business communications. Over the years, we have moved from manual to electric typewriters, then to centralized word-processing centers. During the past three years, every office worker—from clerical to manager—has been given the option of equipping his or her desk with a personal computer and various software packages for word-processing, spreadsheets, graphics, and electronic mail.

Now, TechTile Industries advances beyond letter-quality word-processing to typeset-quality desktop publishing. As a result, every employee can use personal computers to create more effective printed communications on the job.

Desktop publishing combines personal computers, high-quality printers that produce typeset-looking pages, and specialized page layout software. With this three-part system, you can combine word-processed text and computer graphics to design and print professional-looking documents—without leaving your desk.

Radius II Brings Industrial Specs to the Home

Old reliable.

The Radius Series is where TechTile began, and there are over 200,000 commercial installations to prove its durability.

The same qualities found in the Radius Series are part of the Radius II package as well.

But there are differences. The profile of the individual stud has been altered.

The profile is lower for the home setting, but still gives the suggestion of texture.

And color selection is much deeper for the Radius II Series, as are the finishes. Where a high gloss might work well in a kitchen setting, a children's playroom might do better with a semi-transparent surface.

Individual tile sizes have been reduced to 1 square foot to accommodate the smaller total floor area found in private homes.

- height of stud: 4mm

- 15 colors

- individual tile: 1 square foot

- roughened reverse

Look to Quadrille for Color Excitement

A tile made specifically for the home. Lighter weight than an industrial tile. Greater installation flexibility. The hard-wearing surface that remains the backbone of all TechTile products will stand up to the pedestrian and light-wheeled traffic of the home.

The resilient material not only provides a comfortable surface to walk or stand on, it deadens sound. It can be used outdoors as an added safety feature around the pool.

The color range is the most exciting feature for any homeowner. Colors range from the industrial to muted pastels, from electric primaries to earth tones. A choice for any setting, whether formal, functional, casual, or chic. No matter what the wear or weather, the color remains as true as the day the tile was laid.

- 2.7mm and 4mm

- 15 colors

- two-mix epoxy or adhesive

- roughened reverse

To make desktop publishing available to all employees immediately, TechTile Industries is adding desktop publishing workstations to every department in the company. These workstations will be in place only until we can install a desktop publishing system on every employee's desk.

TechTile Industries' Corporate Communications division has prepared this style guide to help you make the most of desktop publishing. *Desktop Publishing With Style* covers guidelines you should follow to:

- create the text and graphics that you want included in your publications

- use page layout software to combine your text and graphics files into publications you create routinely on the job

- whenever possible, use the existing page designs in our company template package to create materials for external use

- if necessary, put in a request for desktop publishing training through the Personal Computing Division

Because desktop publishing offers tremendous flexibility, this section details style guidelines established by TechTile Industries' Corporate Communications division.

Everyone should follow these guidelines so all company publications look consistent with each other and with the overall corporate image.

Setting up temporary workstations for document production

All letters, presentation overheads, reports, and other communications intended for distribution outside TechTile Industries can be produced at the temporary departmental workstations.

First priority for the workstations will go to people producing external documents. As available, the workstations can be used for internal communications, too.

The manager of each department will designate one person to schedule the desktop publishing workstation. That person will also be the initial contact for assessing and reporting equipment malfunctions.

A few standards for company-wide desktop publishing

Each temporary desktop publishing workstation is equipped with a computer — either an Apple Macintosh or a PC-compatible — as well as a hard disk. Most departments have PC-compatible computers because they have been widely used throughout the company for the past three years.

Left. The finished product

Each computer is connected to a PCL printer, or to a PostScript printer, which produces typeset-quality pages. By choosing fonts available on the printer, you can create documents that look as though they have been typeset, not just typed or produced on a letter-quality printer.

For external publications, TechTile Industries uses three type families available on both PCL and PostScript printers:

- Times for the main text of any publication

- Helvetica for headlines, charts, graphs, tables, and statistical data

- Symbol for scientific, special language, and other unique symbols

Other type families may be available on your workstationUs printer. Limit those other type families to internal and special purpose publications.

If you do not know how to use this equipment, read Bulletin 24, RTroubleshooting and Training,S to enroll in an introductory computer course taught by the Personal Computing division.

Getting to know your desktop publishing software

On each computer, TechTile IndustriesU Personal Computing Division has installed all the applications you need for desktop publishing:

- Aldus PageMaker, a desktop publishing application you use to combine word-processing and graphics files as you design your documents page by page

- Various word-processing applications chosen because they are already used throughout TechTile Industries and because they all create files that you can use with PageMaker

- Graphics and spreadsheet software that you can use to create a wide variety of charts, drawings, art, and other illustrations, which you save as files that you can add to your PageMaker documents

Each workstation includes documentation for all software packages. Most packages include tutorials that cover all the basic skills needed for most tasks.

If you want additional training on any of this software, read Bulletin 24, RTroubleshooting and Training,S for a list of training sessions available through the Personal Computing division.

Maintaining other corporate standards in your daily work

Desktop publishing may have revolutionized page-layout and general document preparation, but effective communication also depends on the power of the written word.

Our desktop publishing workstations will be equipped with copies of the **TechTile Style Guide.**

Use Tech Tile Style Guide to ensure that your materials not only look good, but are written correctly, clearly and succinctly.

Desktop Systems Corp.

For further information contact
Desktop Systems Corp.
All correspondence should be addressed to:
Public Relations
Desktop Systems Corporation
P.O. Box 0001
ATLANTIS

Text and graphic placeholders

We have mentioned that a template can contain any amount of graphics or text you like. If we consider a monthly newsletter, the actual content of this newsletter will change from month to month. One would think, therefore, we cannot include much text in the template, as it will have to be updated anyway. However, by using text and graphics as "placeholders" we can include as much text and graphics in our template as we need without having to worry about this text being removed or updated. Using text and graphics placeholders in templates makes creating a publication a much easier task.

Let's say that we loaded in one major text file, several graphics files, and several headings throughout our Newsletter Template example. When we open up the template next month, the graphics, text, and headings are all there, but we now have new text, graphics, and headings that are going to replace those of last month. Replacing the old text with the new becomes very easy, and the process of replacing the old text and graphics helps us to precisely format and position the new elements.

Graphic placeholders

In a simple copy of a newsletter template of Figure 12, let's choose to first replace the old graphics on the first page with a new graphic. Select the old graphic that is going to be replaced, immediately before selecting the *Place* command (Figures 13 and 14). When you do choose the *Place* command, locate the new graphic as in Figure 15 and select it, but do not yet choose OK.

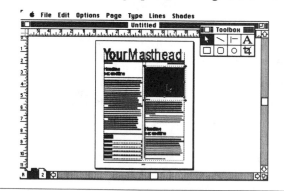

Figure 12. To work through with us in this section of the module load the Newsletter template contained in the PageMaker Templates folder. As shown in this figure, it contains various text and graphics place-holders on Page 1. We have selected the graphic in the top right-hand corner to be replaced.

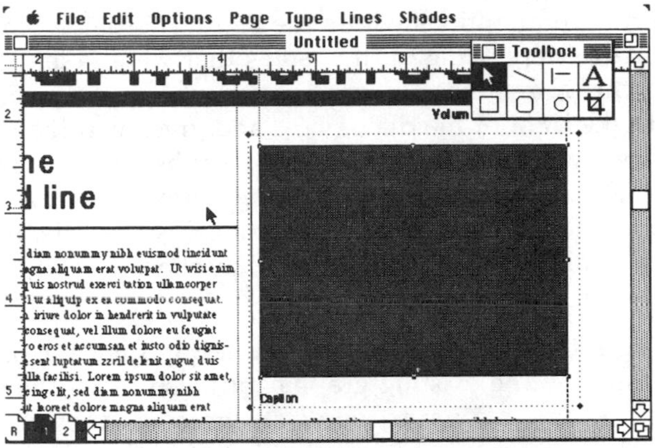

Figure 13. We have changed to Actual size view so that you can see how the graphic we have selected is going to be replaced

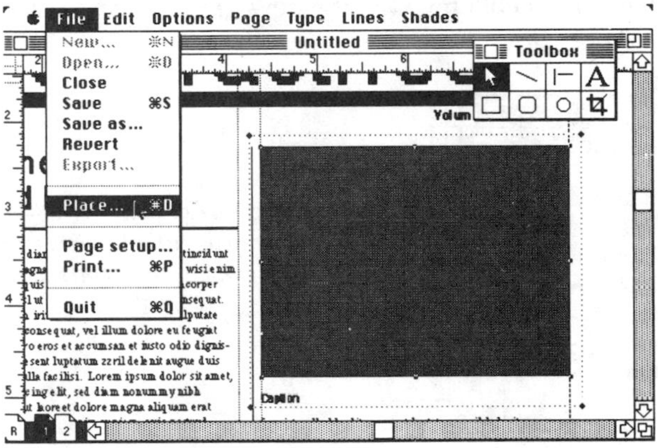

Figure 14. With the graphic still selected, we choose the Place command from the **File** menu to locate the new graphic.

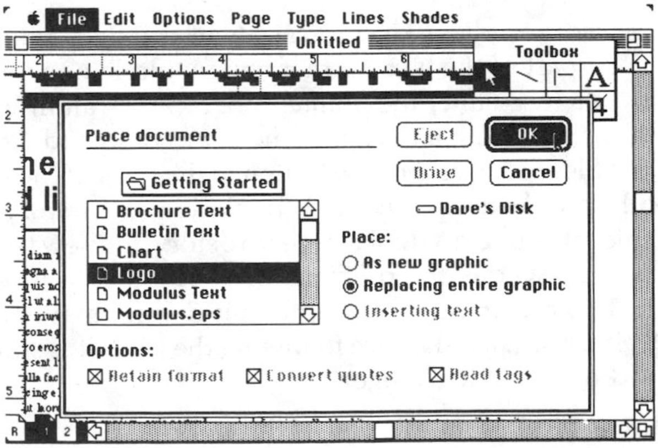

Figure 15. The graphic we are going to use to replace the old graphic is Logo. Note that we also select the option to the right — Replacing entire graphic (see the explanation on the next page).

There are several options within the Figure 15 dialog box that may be active depending on the steps that were taken before choosing this command. The one that should be active now is located to the right of the dialog box, and gives you the choice between two ways to load the graphic — either *As new graphic*, which is selected by default, or *Replacing entire graphic*. As new graphic is a picture loaded in the traditional way — the mouse cursor will change appearance and you may choose where to load the graphic on the page.

Replacing entire graphic will insert the new graphic not only in the same area as the existing graphic, but also using the same sizing, cropping, and wraparound attributes as the previous graphic. This can, of course, be modified after the graphic has been replaced. On clicking OK, the new graphic totally replaces the old (Figure 16).

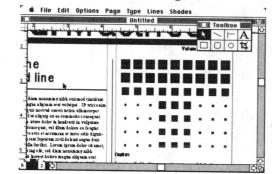

Figure 16. On choosing OK, the new graphic entirely replaces the old, taking on all its attributes.

Text placeholders

The same theory applies to text replacement as it does to graphics. Select any part of the text file that you would like to replace with a new file (use either the pointer tool or make an insertion point with the text tool), and choose the *Place* command. Locate the new text file, and note the new option to the right of the list of files. It will read "As new story" and "Replacing entire story." As with graphics, if you select Replacing entire story, the new text file will completely overlay the previous file — following its exact path. If the files are of different length, this doesn't matter — as there will either be a blank space following the file if it is shorter, or more text to flow if it is longer.

See Figures 17 to 19 for examples of this approach.

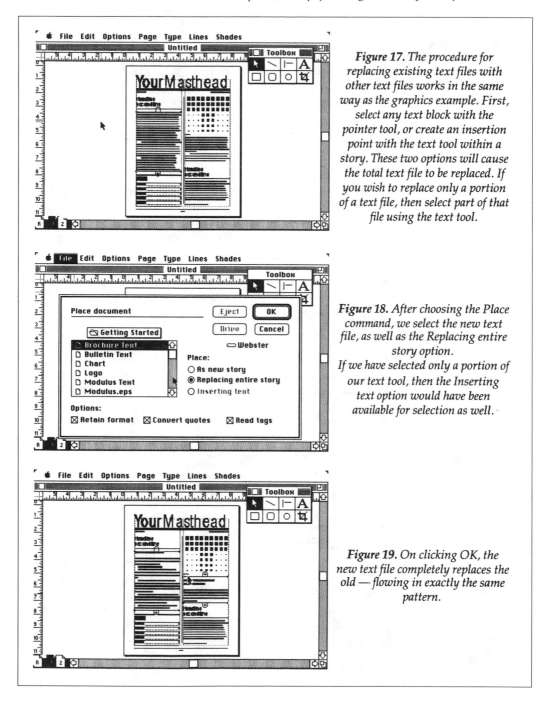

Figure 17. The procedure for replacing existing text files with other text files works in the same way as the graphics example. First, select any text block with the pointer tool, or create an insertion point with the text tool within a story. These two options will cause the total text file to be replaced. If you wish to replace only a portion of a text file, then select part of that file using the text tool.

Figure 18. After choosing the Place command, we select the new text file, as well as the Replacing entire story option.
If we have selected only a portion of our text tool, then the Inserting text option would have been available for selection as well.

Figure 19. On clicking OK, the new text file completely replaces the old — flowing in exactly the same pattern.

Heading placeholders

Heading placeholders work in a slightly different way to other text placeholders. Because headings are generally much shorter than text files, three or four words usually, it is much quicker to type them in PageMaker rather than in a word processor. Let's say, for example, that you have a heading in place in your template as shown in Figure 20.

Simply select the text cursor, and highlight the entire heading (Figure 20). Without pressing the Delete key, or using the *Cut* command, type in the new heading. The new heading will completely overwrite the old, yet use exactly the same attributes (Figure 21). The same type style, justification, and spacing will be applied to the new text.

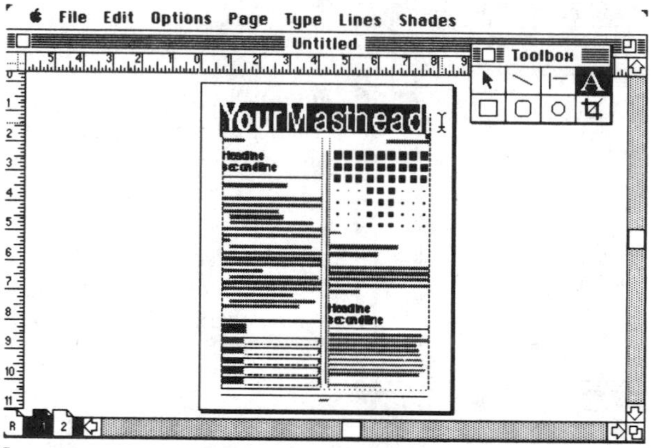

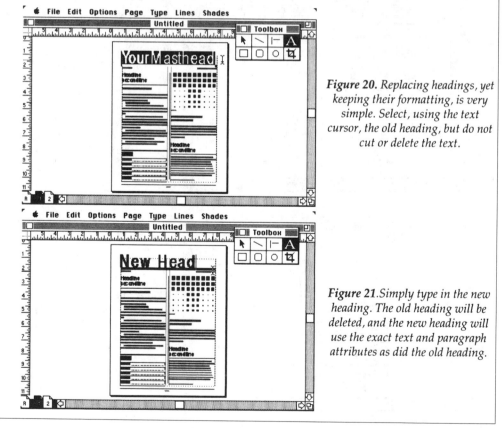

Figure 20. *Replacing headings, yet keeping their formatting, is very simple. Select, using the text cursor, the old heading, but do not cut or delete the text.*

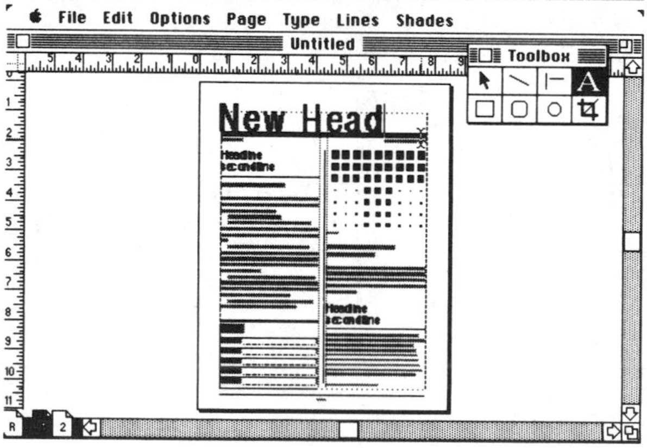

Figure 21.*Simply type in the new heading. The old heading will be deleted, and the new heading will use the exact text and paragraph attributes as did the old heading.*

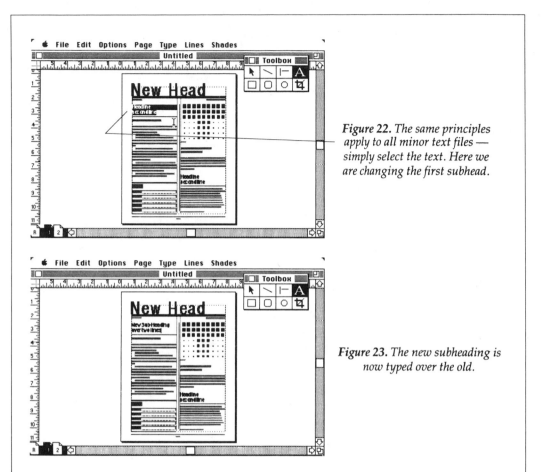

Figure 22. *The same principles apply to all minor text files — simply select the text. Here we are changing the first subhead.*

Figure 23. *The new subheading is now typed over the old.*

All text and graphics placeholders can be regular or simulated. Provided with PageMaker are several "dummy" files that can be used to create a template, so that real files do not have to be created and used.

Chapter 9
Guidelines for Press Releases

Chapter 9
Guidelines for Press Releases

The major objective of a press release is to get editorial coverage in popular industry publications and newspapers. The release should be done on company letterhead and preferably on separate "Press Release" or "News Release" stationery.

There are several different (and satisfactory) ways of preparing press releases. (See example on page 140.)

Under the News (or Press) Release heading should be the subject of the release—in bold type and preferably around 18 point in size. Below this should be two minor headings in bold type:

- **Release Date:**
- **Contact Name**:

With press releases, put the major parts of the announcement in the first paragraph. This is the one that editors will read first and determine whether the product is worth reporting on. Use lots of white space. Start the first paragraph of your story about halfway down the page.

Always use double line spacing for press releases. This gives editors more room to modify and edit the release. If there's not enough room, it will be thrown out.

The second, third, and subsequent paragraphs should progressively move to less important and, generally, more technical information. Don't make a news release too long—this is also an editorial turn-off. Make sure all pages are numbered.

If you have multiple products being released at the same time, make separate press releases for each. One summary press release could also be written with an overview of the product announcements.

Included at the end of the release should be the company contact name and phone number, and the PR agency contact and phone number (if appropriate).

Chapter 9 Exercise
Guidelines for Press Releases

In this exercise we will set up a template and paragraph styles for the press release example illustrated below. We will then show how this can be used on a continuous basis to quickly produce future press release information.

Desktop Publishing View ← *Constant*

Press Release ← *Constant*

(The above two constants would, in many cases, be included as part of pre-printed stationery)

Self-paced training books for Desktop Publishing

Release Date: ← *January 1989* ← *Variable*
Constant
Contact Name: ← *Mr Joe Pittioni* ← *Variable*
(61 2) 787 8788 *Constant*

Desktop Publishing View is a company that has been very heavily involved in Desktop Publishing since its inception, initially in a consulting and training role, but currently in more of a development and distribution role.

Variable text (should be double-spaced)

Recently Desktop Publishing View announced the release (through M&T) of two new books, PageMaker By Example and Dynamics of Desktop Publishing Design (based on Pagemaker application). These two books are now available at leading book retailers.

They both apply self-paced training and are essential for any Pagemaker user.

Figure 1.
All the Constants are the features that could be contained in a Press Release Template Publication. The Variables are pieces of information that obviously change from press release to press release. It is quite possible, however, to leave these variables in a template, so that they can quickly and easily be deleted to make way for new information. The purpose of their existence then is to save space for the new information, and also in a way pre-tagging the area. This will save your having to alter paragraph styles when creating press releases.

Setting up a template

As mentioned on the previous page, a sample press release can easily be set up. However, because press releases have such a uniformity among them, we can even go one step further than that and create a master template publication. Initially, a press release would be set up in the normal way—the page layout determined, the text entered and paragraph styles created and applied. Let's do that first.

1. Create a new template. Give it the following parameters:

(i)   Letter page size

(ii)   Margins of 1.0 inch all around

(iii)   One column

(iv)   Save as a Template titled PressRel.PT3 (the extension .PT3 being for PageMaker PC users).

On page 1, type in the press information as illustrated in Figure 2.

Desktop Publishing View
  Press Release
  Self-paced training books
for Desktop Publishing
  Release Date:
  January 1989
  Contact Name:
  Mr Joe Pittioni
(61 2) 787 8788

Desktop Publishing View is a company that has been very heavily involved in Desktop Publishing since its inception, initially in a consulting and training role, but currently in more of a development and distribution role.

Recently Desktop Publishing View announced the release (through M&T) of two new books, PageMaker by Example and Dynamics of Desktop Publishing Design (based on Pagemaker application).These two books are now available through leading book retailers.

They both apply self-paced training and are essential for any Pagemaker user.

Figure 2.
Simply type in all the details and create the different paragraph styles. You may prefer to create the styles as you go along—others find it easier to create them at the end.

2. Create and apply new paragraph styles.

We have created a number of new styles from Body Text. These have produced the page layout as shown in Figure 3. You may like yours to be a little different, but Figure 3 illustrates the result of our page once we have applied the new paragraph styles.

When creating the styles, remember the basic guidelines discussed at the beginning of this chapter regarding font size and white space. Remember also that Body Text, or the major subject matter of the press release, should be double-spaced to allow for easy material changes by editors.

After applying all paragraph styles, save your template.

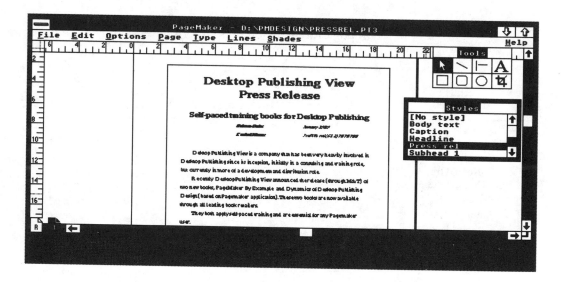

Figure 3.
We have created and applied several new paragraph styles for this press release template. The two headlines created at the top of the page may already exist as part of the company letterhead.

3. Create a new press release from an old one.

When it is time for another press release to be created, all we now have to do is reopen the template publication, and PageMaker will automatically open an untitled copy of the template. All you need do is save it with a new name.

By deleting sections one at a time, each one retains its style information. This template approach streamlines the creation of new press releases even further. It will only take minutes to create a fully laid out and entered press release.

The first change to make on the new press release is the Announcement itself.

Select this text now .

4. Insert new subject matter in the new press release.

Where the subheading "Self-paced training books for Desktop Publishing" is now selected, type in the new heading "Dynamics of Desktop Publishing Design"

The other changes to the subject matter are illustrated in Figure 4. Type these in now.

Desktop Publishing View
 Press Release
 Dynamics of Desktop Publshing Design
 Release Date:
 May 18, 1989
 Contact Name:
 Mr Joe Pittioni (61 2} 787 8788

 Due to the unprecedented demand of the recently released book
'Dynamics of Desktop Publishing Design, the 40,000 copies originally
printed have sold out. A new edition will be available from June 1, 1989.

Figure 4.
The new text to be included in the second press release.

Notice the ease at which you can change the previous press release, by utilizing the preformatted styles and typing in the new subject details over the old.

Figure 5.
Our template press release has been duplicated for use as a new press release.

Note: For simple one or two-page press releases, there is no real advantage in typing first into a word processor and then importing this text into PageMaker.

For longer documents, we can still open this template as an untitled copy, and adjust the announcement headline, release date, and contact name, as suggested above.

By using options under the *Place* command, such as "Replacing entire story," new body text information can be brought in and can replace the main body of text that has been selected with the cursor.

This is an optional method to replacing the body text component, and is more suitable than straight text type over for large amounts of copy. (Refer to pages 130 to 135 for more information on text and graphic placeholders.)

Page numbers should be added if your press release is more than one page.

Chapter 10
Guidelines for Overhead Transparencies

Chapter 10
Guidelines for Overhead Transparencies

Presentations to groups of people can be done for a variety of reasons—selling, motivating, informing, or entertaining. In situations involving selling and informing, a well-designed series of overhead transparencies can go a long way towards reinforcing the theme of a presentation. In this example, we will consider the case of preparing overhead presentations for a selling environment.

Why do overhead transparencies assist in presentation giving? The major reasons are:

- *Increases audience understanding and saves time. A picture or chart can be a much better way of presenting information. Your message will get across in a shorter period of time.*

- *Enhances company image. Well-developed slides can make you and your company look more professional.*

- *Increases retention. Effective overhead charts allow the audience to absorb and retain more information.*

- *Allows key presentation topics to be more easily highlighted.*

- *The acceptance of a presenter's ideas is better with visuals.*

- *The impact on the decision-making process is improved. Research shows you are twice as likely to get a favorable decision if you use visuals, and you will cut down the meeting length by about a quarter.*

Important points to consider when designing overhead transparencies are as follows:

- Design your text and graphics to fit in a rectangle using a 3:4 ratio (with the longer of the two sides horizontal—i.e., landscape format). The rectangle may be non-printing or printing. If printing, a rectangle combined with a company logo is quite effective.

- If you are designing presentations to be later photographed and used within 35 mm slides, then a 2:3 ratio is required.

- Keep all overhead charts simple—one to two major points at most, supported by several minor points. Use bullets, wherever possible, to present relevant points.

- Where possible, keep all text in upper and lowercase. One or two word headings may be in uppercase only.

- Text may be serif or sans serif style. Research has shown little difference in audience comprehension.

- Make sure all slides are consistent—same font size and styles.

- The addition of color may be helpful in enhancing particular points. Color printers and plotters may be used with PageMaker to enhance your presentation.

- Keep all text towards the top of the slide. Overhead projectors have a major problem with physical intrusions, sometimes stopping part of the audience from effectively reading the information. The higher the text, the more easily it will be seen.

- Keep type size as large as possible, say 18 to 24 point, to ensure slides are readable at a distance.

- If in a selling environment, highlight benefits of your product, not features. Benefits sell, features may confuse the customer.

Good and bad examples

Figures 1 and 2 indicate badly designed overhead transparencies for the reasons as discussed in the captions. Figures 3 and 4 are acceptable presentation charts.

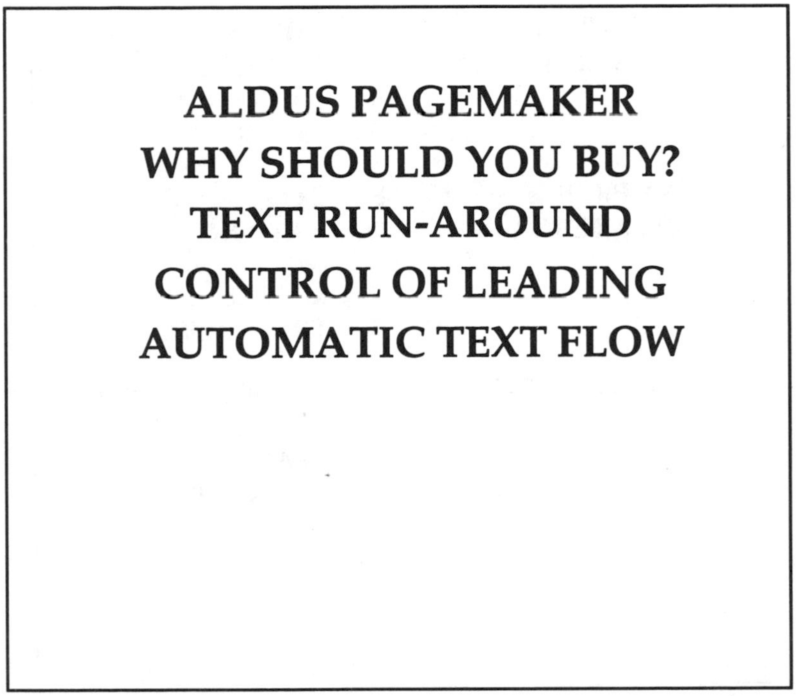

ALDUS PAGEMAKER
WHY SHOULD YOU BUY?
TEXT RUN-AROUND
CONTROL OF LEADING
AUTOMATIC TEXT FLOW

Figure 1.
This slide is not acceptable for the following reasons:

(i) All text is in uppercase, and therefore harder to read.
(ii) Hard to define which point is which without use of bullets.
(iii) Only features are highlighted—no benefits. This may confuse the prospects.

ALDUS PAGEMAKER
REASONS FOR BUYING

FEATURES	BENEFITS
WIDE VARIETY OF RULING LINES	IMPROVES LAYOUT QUALITY BUILDS VISUAL INTEREST
MANY PRESET TEMPLATES	EASE OF OPERATION
	INCREASES PRODUCTIVITY
FIVE PAGE VIEWS	INCREASES LAYOUT CONTROL INCREASES PRODUCTIVITY EASE OF OPERATION

Figure 2.
This slide is not acceptable for the following reasons:

(i) All text is in uppercase, and therefore harder to read.
(ii) Too many points on one chart.
(iii) Doesn't fit into 3:4 rectangular ratio.
(iv) Last three or four lines may not be seen by audience.
(Compare this to the presentation chart shown in Figure 4.)

ALDUS PAGEMAKER
Why should you buy?

- **Will save you money**

- **Will save you time**

- **Provides increased layout flexibility**

- **Easily integrates text & graphics**

Figure 3.
This is an acceptable overhead transparency for the following reasons:

(i) Except for the top heading, all text is upper and lowercase.
(ii) Only four points are highlighted per chart.
(iii) Bullets are used to highlight points.
(iv) Benefits of product (not features) are highlighted.
(v) 3:4 rectangular ratio is utilized.
(vi) Border adds more formality to chart.

ALDUS PAGEMAKER
Reasons For Buying?

Features	Benefits
• **Wide variety of ruling lines**	• **Improves layout quality**
	• **Builds visual interest**
• **Many preset templates**	• **Ease of operation**
	• **Increases productivity**

Figure 4.
This is an acceptable chart and a redone version of Figure 2. Note the differences.
Figure 4 is favored because:

(i) Upper and lowercase text.
(ii) Less text on chart—only two major points are included.
(iii) Border allows features and benefits to be more easily comprehended.
(iv) Bullets are used to emphasize major points.

Guidelines for
Overhead Transparencies

By going through steps 1 to 10 below, you will be able to set up a master page within a template document, incorporating the use of paragraph styles designed exactly for your requirements.

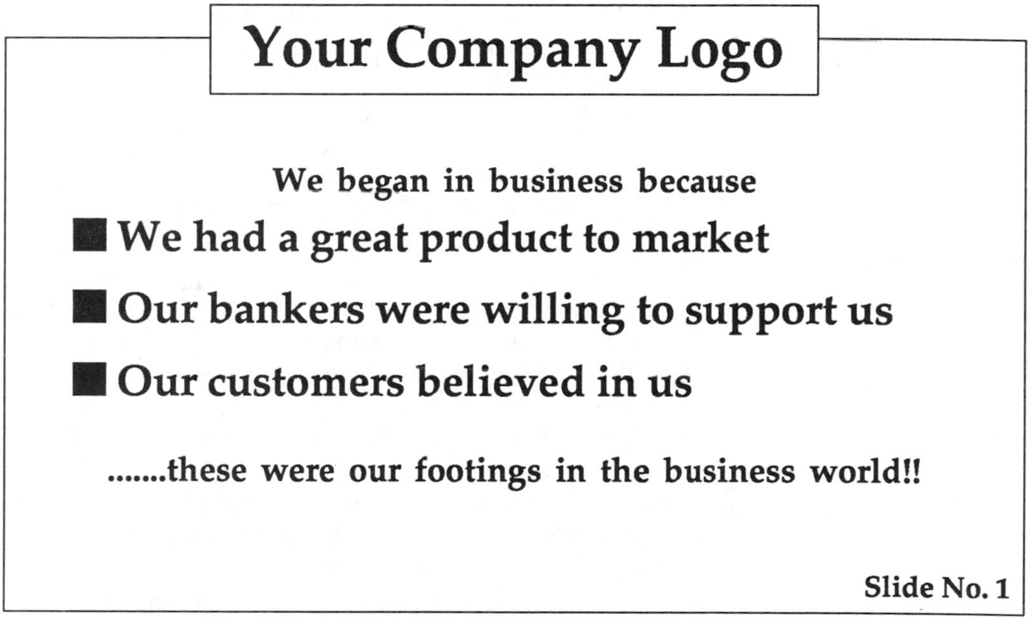

Your Company Logo

We began in business because

■ **We had a great product to market**

■ **Our bankers were willing to support us**

■ **Our customers believed in us**

.......these were our footings in the business world!!

Slide No. 1

Figure 5.
This is the overhead template we will create.
Remember, when creating the 3:4 ratio for the overhead, that what appears on the screen can often be deceptive.

1. Open a new document. Save as a template and call it Exer1.PT3. Use only a single sided page setup.

2. Go to the master page to create your repeating information. Set up margins and page size to your requirements bearing in mind the 3:4 ratio must be maintained.

3. Type in, or place, your Company logo and select the type size, font, and alignment specifications. This will repeat on every page.

4. Using the square corner drawing tool, create a box on the page similar to the one in Figure 5. Create another smaller box, to accommodate the company logo.

5. Type in the words Slide No. and implement PageMaker's automatic numbering feature, for the actual number. Position this block of text at the bottom right hand corner of the frame, as indicated in Figure 5.

What you have created so far is the base layout. Different information can now be inserted on each overhead transparency, however, the standard format will remain the same on each page throughout the series that you are about to create.

6. Go to the first page of the template which should reflect your master page. Enter the remaining text in the frame similar to Figure 5. The square bullet command used for this example is created by typing in 'n' then selecting the Zapf Dingbats type face. You may wish to vary this.
Remember, no more than three or four major points per chart.

7. Select the first line with the text tool. Go to *Define styles* under the **Type** menu. Select 'New' and base it on Subhead 2. Call it Subhead 3. Go into 'Type' and select point size and type face. Go into 'Para' and center text. Once this is complete, if you select *Style Palette* under the **Options** menu you will be able to select any text and apply any style to this text. Now select the next three lines and create a new style following the above steps to make it similar to text in Figure 5. Do the same with the last line.

8. Insert one more page. Go back to page 1, select all text, copy, and paste onto page 2. You will have to position the text after it has been pasted using ruler guides for accuracy.

   Next time you open this document it will automatically create a new untitled document leaving the original template unopened. You are free to edit and change text within this format, but Master Page components can only be edited on the Master page.

9. Go to page 2. Type in the detailed contents of Figure 6. By typing over what has been pasted onto page two, you do not have to re-apply paragraph styles. The correct style attributes will automatically apply

Figure 6.
The slide on your second page should look similar to this on completion.

10. If you are not happy with basic layouts and would like to highlight points further, by all means experiment as much as possible. For maximum audience comprehension, remember that your presentations should maintain at all times simplicity and consistency.

Note that the PageMaker software for both PC and Macintosh do have sample overhead templates within the templates directory or folder.

Chapter 11
Display Headlines

Chapter 11
Display Headlines

Using attention getters

Often headlines are thrust upon the designer, and you have to do the best with what you've got. Often, also, the headlines are too long to be set in one line, and it is necessary to divide them into two, three, or more lines.

There are a number of ways a headline can be grouped, depending on certain considerations which vary from publication to publication.

One of the best groupings is to have the headline form an inverted pyramid. This has the effect of leading the eye into the text.

The regular pyramid points upwards and tends to lead the eye away from the text. It should not be used unless there is an important illustration above the headline. Even then it's questionable.

Staggered headlines, with each line slightly to the right of the line above it, are useful in displays. Here it is more important that each line be approximately the same length, or the headline will be unbalanced.

Squared-off headlines are acceptable in any type of design, forming a well-proportioned rectangle.

One of the most popular methods is to let the lines fall as they will, with the longest line in the display at the top. This fits the requirement that we direct the eye towards the text.

Common sense also comes into play. Sometimes a meaning can be altered radically by turning words onto another line. A classic example:

Soviet Virgin Lands
Short Of Goal Again

or

Soviet Virgin
Lands Short Of
Goal Again

A common dictum is that headings should be set flush left. While flush left is neat and tidy, it sometimes looks incongruous in a conventional design.

It is, however, becoming an element of modern design principles, which we will look at in a later chapter.

Figure 1 shows examples of the headline groupings discussed.

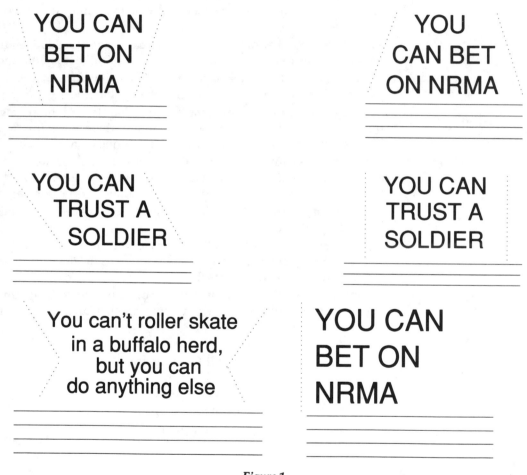

Figure 1.
Examples of headline groupings.

Breaking headlines

There are techniques within PageMaker that allow you to effectively control headlines.

To break a headline, a carriage return is inserted at the point of the break.

However, in Figures 2 and 3 you will notice that whenever a carriage return is inserted in the headline, any space before or after that headline is used for the new paragraph we have just created.

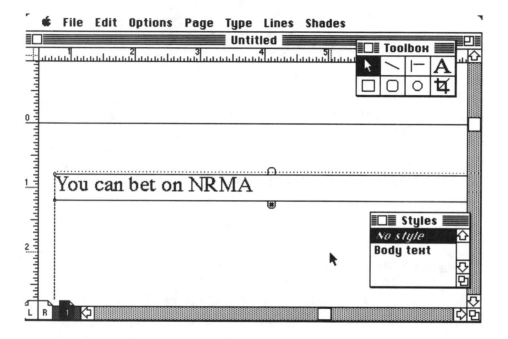

Figure 2.
In this example we want to break this headline at "bet." If we insert the text cursor at "bet..."

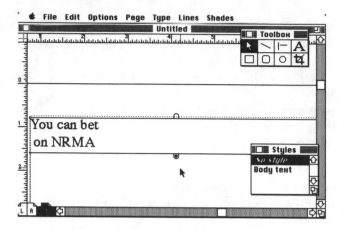

Figure 3.

... and insert a return, we get all the spacing assigned before or after the heading's paragraph style (if there is any), before and after our new paragraph as well.

To resolve this, you simply need to alter the paragraph style (rename it if necessary), and remove all the space before and after in the paragraph command.

When large fonts are used, it may also be necessary to manually change the leading to a size equal to the font. By changing this it will help to avoid unnecessary white space between headline text.

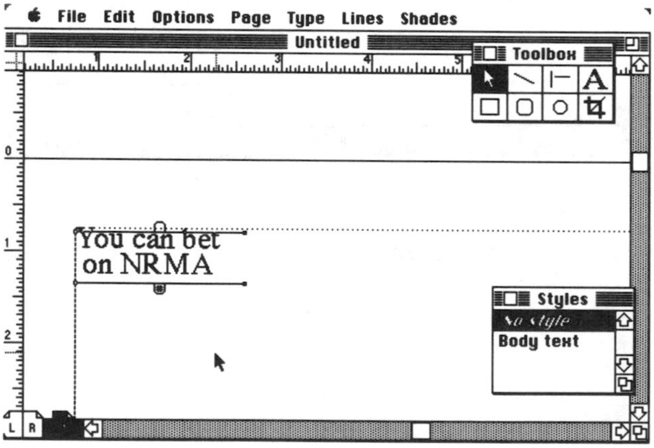

Figure 4.

Change the leading of the heading in question to equal the font size and the result will be a more effective heading.

Changing headline widths

There are several options within Pagemaker that can alter the width of headlines. The first, and perhaps the most important, design-wise, is *Pair kerning*.

In the Paragraph specifications dialog box, Pair kerning is always activated, by default, to text above 12 points (Figure 5).

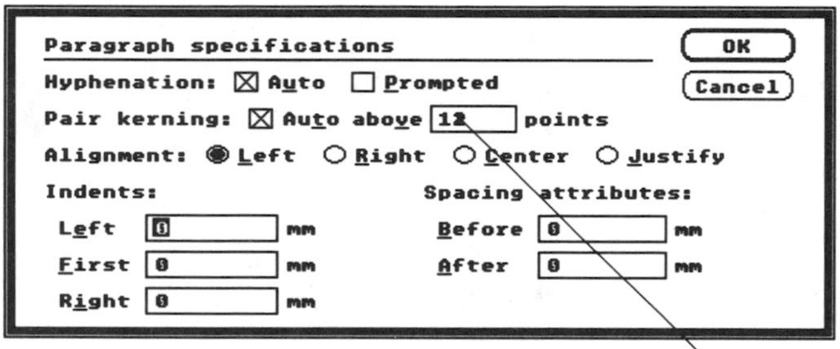

Figure 5.
Paragraph specifications dialog box showing Pair kerning set for above 12 points

To manually kern two characters (to add or delete 1/48th EM space) place the text cursor between the two characters:

To *add* space (for Mac users) press Command + Shift + Delete keys. To *delete* space press Command + Delete keys.

To *add* space (for PC compatible users) press Control + Shift + Backspace keys. To *delete* space press Control + Backspace keys.

Another alternative to kerning headlines is to actually insert an extra space between the letters and words with the spacebar. This can be used for added effect if there is only one or two words.

Chapter 12
Directing Eye Movement

Chapter 12
Directing Eye Movement

"Stars" and focal points

Every layout should have its outstanding unit or center of interest. In other words—a "star."

Before starting thumbnail sketches for a layout, the designer should study the copy and select a star. It may be a picture of the product or a snappy headline. The star should then be positioned where it will make impact and lead the reader into the main text, or message.

Keep in mind what research discovered about the way people read. The eye starts at the top-left corner, before leaping to the focal point in the upper-third of the page. It then passes downwards and to the right, ending somewhere in the lower-quarter of the page on the right-hand side.

The *focal point* is then the best place to locate the most important part of the layout. Just below the focal point is the *field*, where it is necessary to hold the eye of the reader, so it won't pass on and out of the page. This is where we can place subheadings, or the text itself. It is essential that the reader's eye be guided through the field, without interruption, to the fringe, the lower part of the display which contains the name of the advertiser or product.

Figure 1 provides an example of this approach.

There are some differing opinions about the use of white space. Some insist that white space is important. So it is—if used correctly. However, it can also destroy a layout if used improperly. If you place a large amount of white space between the focal point and the field, or between the field and the fringe, the white space explodes the design, and the reader's attention is lost. White space is great in its place—and that is to frame your work.

White space is as much a graphic as any black. A good layout harmonizes the contrast between black and white.

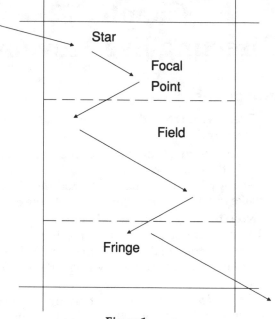

Figure 1.
Stars and focal points.

Pointing devices

Sometimes it is advantageous to help readers from the focal point of a design to the field, and then to the fringe. This can be done using *pointing devices* such devices as hands, arrows, and lines.

Research does show, however, that more subtle pointing devices than arrows can have the same effect. The eye follows the direction of travel and sight.

For example, if we have a picture of a person, with the eyes looking into the page, the reader's eyes will do likewise. Similarly, a picture of a car travelling into the page will entice the reader to do likewise. Conversely, a picture of an object pointing out of the page will drag the reader's eyes away from the intended direction, and the text may go unread.

See Figures 2 and 3 following for good and bad examples of this technique.

Figure 2.
In this example, the runner and the shoes point out of the page. This is not effective.

Figure 3.
In this case, both the runner and the shoes point into the page. This is much more effective.

Rotating and flipping images

When using images to guide the eye of the reader, remember that these images cannot be rotated in any way by PageMaker. Consequently, you must either go back to the package that your image was created in (which should allow you to rotate the picture), or just be careful where you place the image on the page.

PageMaker pointing devices

PageMaker does not allow you to create arrows from the toolbox. Larger arrows can be accessed through Clip Art libraries or can be created in a graphics package, then stored in a Clip Art file for easy access. Figure 4 below illustrates an example of some useful arrows.

The Zapf Dingbats font can be used, as shown in Figure 5, to produce a range of pointing devices.

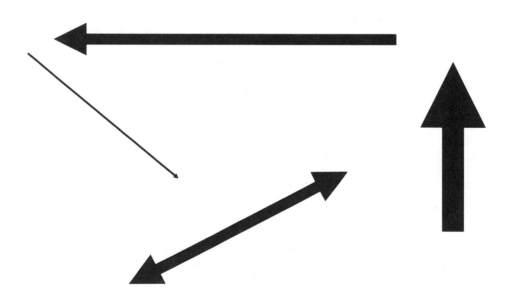

Figure 4.
Some pointing tools that can be used within PageMaker, but accessed from outside graphics packages.

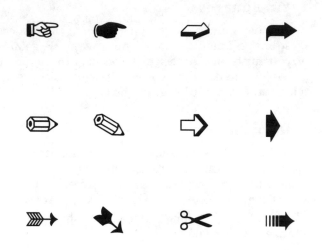

Figure 5.
Pointing devices available with the Zapf Dingbats font.

Chapter 13
Illustrations

Chapter 13
Illustrations

When and where to use illustrations

You may be confronted, at some stage, with the need to incorporate several illustrations into a design. This can cause more problems than all other design features put together.

It is simple to put, say, six illustrations in a neat rectangle at the head of a page. Sometimes this isn't practical as the illustrations are different sizes and shapes and don't go together readily. This leads to a strong temptation to place illustrations throughout the text.

This is where problems arise with reader's comprehension and concentration. By placing illustrations throughout the text, we are, in effect, asking the reader to make a decision every time he/she comes to one—do I jump over the picture and continue reading on, or do I jump to the head of the next column? The illustration is a natural barrier, and the reader has to decide how to go ahead.

Research has shown this to be one of the great turn-offs for readers. The moral here seems to be: don't do it. There is always a better way.

NRMA Leaflets—How Many Are Read?

Executive Summary

The NRMA (National Roads and Motorists's Association) is Australia's largest motoring organization. It is also involved in a wide range of insurance including car, boat and house. The study contained in this chapter was undertaken to determine the extent to which NRMA leaflets are read by members. It was conducted by the Publications Editor, Colin Wheildon, between November 1985 and August 1987.

The study, of 24 product marketing and community service leaflets, covered leaflets distributed to target audiences and leaflets mailed directly to members, such as by bulk mail or in-serted in the NRMA's magazine - *The Open Road*. The main findings of the study were:-

At best, one in three members will read an NRMA leaflet, even when the members are in a target audience (that is, they have declared interest in the subject, and may have requested a leaflet). On average, the readership of NRMA targeted leaflets is one in four; at worst one in twelve (Figure 1).

Very little difference was recorded between readership of marketing and com-

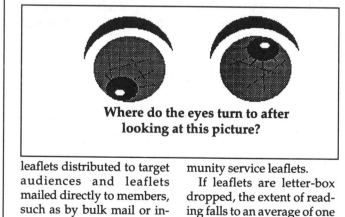

Where do the eyes turn to after looking at this picture?

munity service leaflets.

If leaflets are letter-box dropped, the extent of reading falls to an average of one in 20, with a high of one in 10 and a low of one in 100 (Figure 2).

The low readership of letter-box dropped leaflets prevented meaningful comparison between leaflets distributed in this manner. Therefore all data in this study which invite comparison refer to leaflets aimed at target audiences.

One in two readers will read the headline of a leaflet and no further, irrespective of whether the leaflet is targeted or delivered gratuitously; of the subject of the leaflet; of design features; or of length of text. There is, however, no guarantee that because a headline is read it will be understood and the message of the leaflet comprehended.

While the number of words in a leaflet is not a factor in its readability, the size and style of the type used, and the design of the leaflet, can have considerable bearing on the reader's willingness and ability to read and comprehend the message.

Figure 1.
The picture in columns 1 and 2 forms a barrier to the reading of the text. Some people will jump over this and go to the top of the next column, others will continue reading down. In either case, confusion can occur.

Computer-generated graphics

As you will have already noticed, the graphics tools in PageMaker are certainly not designed for any serious creative graphics. They are fine for outlines, underlines, simple forms and graphs, but for anything more complex, another program must be used.

Do not, however, fall into the trap of considering that all computer-generated art is unworthy of high-quality publications. Obviously, the quality of the graphics will differ from program to program, but on the next few pages we will look at several examples from many of the third-party packages that can be used with PageMaker on the PC.

Some of these pictures have been scanned in via an optical scanner, several have been generated totally on the computer, and several involve a mixture of these two techniques. All pictures that are shown on this and the following pages can be brought into PageMaker and adjusted from there. When we say adjusted, we mean they can be manipulated in size and moved anywhere on the page. They cannot be flipped, rotated, reverse imaged, or anything too fancy, within PageMaker.

PC Paintbrush (image)

Figure 2.
Both of these pictures have been created using PC Paintbrush, which creates a PCX file on the PC. This package is called an image package by PageMaker, meaning that it produces a bit-mapped image. As the picture is increased in size, the resolution is decreased. Usually the maximum resolution for this package is 300 dpi.

CorelDRAW (EPSF Line-art)

Figure 3.

These graphics are imported from a package that runs on the PC called Corel Draw. These particular files are EPSF (PostScript) files, they can only be used by owners of PostScript Printers (although other Corel Draw file formats apart from EPSF, can be printed on other printers). These images can be rescaled and resized without sacrificing resolution. They will also print at whatever the resolution of the printer may be (up to 2540 dpi for a typesetter).

Macintosh drawing files(PICT)

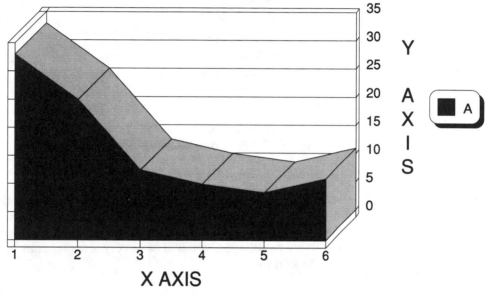

TITLE

SUBTITLE

Figure 4.
This picture was produced in Cricket Draw. Macintosh drawing packages are able to produce files as Pict line-art files. They can be printed on any printer, and like PostScript files, they can be resized and rescaled without ever sacrificing resolution. They will also print at the resolution of the output device.

On the previous few pages, we saw examples of the three major different types of graphics PageMaker can use: bit-mapped images, PostScript, and line-art. You must make sure that the package you use to create your graphics is compatible with PageMaker, as PageMaker can accept both images and line-art in a variety of formats. Many packages will allow you to convert to any one of these formats:

- *Line-art:*
  - Adobe Illustrator 88
  - Cricket Draw
  - MacDraw
  - CorelDraw
  - Video Show
  - Encapsulated PostScript Format (EPSF)

- *Image*
  - Macintosh Paint Files
  - PC Paintbrush
  - Tag Image File Format (TIFF)

Macintosh graphics packages provide several format options to store the graphic data, depending on which environment you wish to take the picture into. If you stay with the formats mentioned in the above paragraphs, you will have very few problems bringing in your graphic files.

Chapter 14
Borders and Rules

Chapter 14
Borders and Rules

How to use them, when, and where

There are two sorts of borders: plain and fancy.

Years ago, they were used around every page of a book for decoration. Now their use is mainly functional, with some decorative applications.

Their functional use is to separate advertisements from one another, from text, and to separate sections of displays from other sections, or to link design elements. At times they are used to frame text on a page, especially when this text is considered important.

They are at times overused in the functional context, because the desired effect can often be achieved by the judicious use of white space.

If a border is selected for decorative use, the designer should consider the nature of the product and target audience.

A page advertising antique furniture could be suited with a simple decorative rule; a page advertising modern office furniture could be best suited to a single-line rule.

Don't go overboard. If anyone comments on the beautiful rule you have chosen for the publication or display, it is proof that the rule is interfering with the message.

When working with color borders and rules there is one thing to remember—a border printed in color may need to be heavier than if printed in black because color tends to reduce the perceived weight. This does depend upon hue and saturation. It is also true that if we design a rule to be in color, but change our mind and go back to black, we may change the rule to a lighter tone.

A single rule around a design often looks dull, so try parallel or contrasting rules. Of the two, contrasting rules are usually more attractive.

When using a contrasting rule, the lightest weight line should be on the inside, towards the type, as it leads the eye in towards the text.

In PageMaker, borders can be created using the drawing tools in the toolbox. The borders can be defined with the options under the **Line** menu. Borders with rounded corners are more noticable than rectangular ones.

Figures 1 through 5 show some examples of borders and rules produced from within PageMaker. Figures 6 and 7 illustrate borders that can be imported from other packages.

Figure 1.

An example of multiple borders created using the rectangle drawing tool and using a line thickness of 2 points

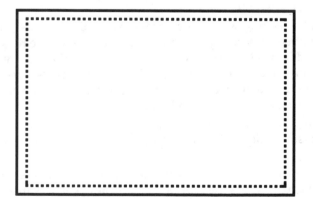

Figure 2.

In this example, we have created two borders similar to the borders in Figure 1, but this time applied different line attributes.

Figure 3.
By selecting the rounded-corner rectangle tool this was produced, and we applied a line thickness of 8 points.

Figure 4.
*This set of ruling lines was produced using the vertical-line drawing tool with the double-line option in the **Lines** menu applied.*

Figure 5.
This shaded box was produced with the rectangle drawing tool and given a fill of 40%.

Imported borders

Some graphics packages often provide border templates—borders that can be imported into PageMaker; borders that are a little more ornate than can be created using PageMaker. You may experiment with creating a few of your own in the graphics packages that are available to you, then store them in your own library.

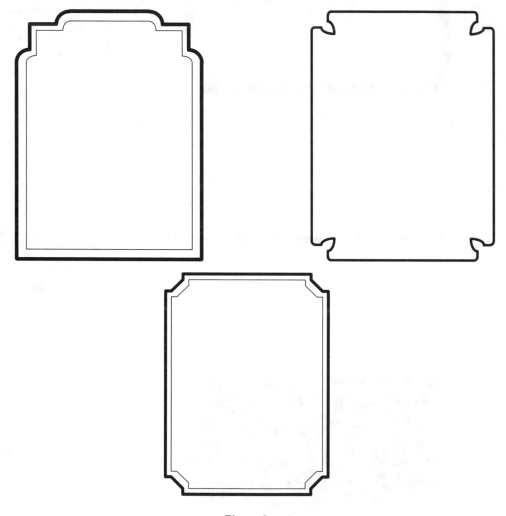

Figure 6.
Some border examples from clip art files

Chapter 15
Guidelines for Books, Manuals, and User Documentation

Chapter 15
Guidelines for Books, Manuals, and User Documentation

Common attributes

Books, manuals, and user documentation have several things in common. They are generally long, require contents, appendices, and indexes, and are normally set in single column width.

PageMaker is well suited to the layout of these publications, with its style sheet and paragraph tagging approach.

Let's first look at what a long document, such as a book, may consist of. Not all such documents will have the same layout, but will be made up from the following list:

- *Title page*
- *Bibliographic and copyright details (on the reverse of the title page)*
- *Foreword*
- *Contents (including pictures, diagrams etc)*
- *Preface (including acknowledgements)*
- *Major text portion of the book*
- *Appendices*
- *Bibliography*
- *Glossary*
- *Index*

The above list can be divided into the three broad areas listed at the top of the next page.

- **Front section:** Title Page, Title Reverse, Foreword, Contents, and Preface

- **Body of publication:** Major text portion

- **Back section**: Appendices, Bibliography, Glossary, and Index

The front section may use lowercase Roman numerals for page numbering. The body of the publication generally uses Arabic numbering in one of two types: standard Arabic numbering starting at 1 and continuing sequentially to the end (the standard approach for a book) or standard arabic numbering, but broken into chapters, such as 1-1 to 1-12, 2-1 to 2-10, etc. (the general approach for manuals, user documentation, and many scientific type reports).

The back section information can be set in the same or smaller text size. Page numbering can continue the normal arabic numbers of a book, or be changed to A-1, B-1, etc.

Let's look now at some details of the different sections.

Title page and reverse. This identifies the title of the publication and the publisher. The title should be set in the same type as the book and is generally centered.

The reverse of the title page provides all the miscellaneous information such as copyright details, ISBN number, original editions, and various reprint information. This page is normally set in the same type style as the book. If a lot of information is included, the type is set at a smaller point size.

Foreword. This is normally written by an outside person—someone in authority to add credibility to the publication. This section varies from one to four pages, and is generally set at the same width and typeface as the body of the book.

Contents. This can be one or more pages long and is designed to assist the reader in finding the section or chapter of interest. It is generally set in the same typeface as the body text, but can be narrower in width for easier reference to page numbers. Some large contents may be set in multiple columns.

Some publications include lists of diagrams, tables, pictures, etc., in the contents. This is probably a subjective decision.

Preface. This is used to provide information on how to use the publication, or details on how or why the publication was produced. Acknowledgements may be included in the Preface if not done separately.

Major text section. This is the body of the book, and can be divided into chapters and, optionally, sections. Most manuals and books are set as one column per page.

Examples of typical page layouts for the body of the book are shown in Figures 1, 2, and 3 on the next page.

Appendices. The appendix or appendices are used to provide supplementary material not always suitable for the general body of the book. Lists are very popular, as are more technical details explaining product operation. The text may be set in slightly smaller type, particularly if name and address lists etc., are included, or the same size type if the information is considered important to the structure of the book.

Headers, footers, and page numbers would be arranged in a similar fashion to the body of the book, as shown in Figure 2.

Bibliography. This is a list of publications, books and other material mentioned throughout the book. It is normally set in a type size smaller than body text.

Glossary. If needed, this is included after the Bibliography. It can be set in two columns and in reduced type.

Index. The Index is an important part of a technical book or user manual. It is normally set in smaller type over two or three columns.

Chapter 1
Desktop Publishing Overview

Introduction

Desktop Publishing began way back in 1985 with the introduction of the Macintosh computer and PageMaker. It was not long before PageMaker was adapted to support the PC world and the results have been staggering. The Desktop Publishing concept is progressively revolutionising the industry.

History of Publishing

There have been three major milestones in the history of publishing. Desktop Publishing obviously has

Figure 1.

This is one of many examples of how the first page of a chapter may commence. Text is set justified and headings are upper and lowercase, as are subheads. The page number is centered at the bottom of the page (not shown).

Desktop Publishing Overview 5

The effect on the corporate business in terms of cost and long term benefits for return on investment are strikingly obvious. All the original sceptics are now beginning to accept that DeskTop Publishing is indeed a revolution to the publishing industry.
Desktop Publishing has been the 'flavour of the month' for well over two years now, illustrating that it is hardly a passing fad in the computer industry. As the months and years pass, virtually all computer users will find themselves tied into desktop publishing one way or another. This will become increasingly true as the cost of peripherals such as lasers,

4 State of the Art Publishing

Gutenberg instigated perhaps the most fundamental of the three great milestones in publishing. Books after Gutenberg became available to the masses - the world was crawling out of the ignorant days of the dark ages.

Benefits of Desktop Publishing

In a similar way, Desktop Publishing has brought the process of publishing to the masses. People who never previously even considered themselves as 'publishers'are finding that desktop publishing has tremendous advantages not the least being money.

Figure 2.

This is a facing page view, following on from Figure 1. The headers include mirror image page numbers (even pages on left, odd pages on right). The book name is on the even page, with the chapter name on the odd or right-hand page. A ruling line below the headers helps to separate the header from the text.

1. Unpacking the Printer

Included in package

Included in your package should be the X456ds laser printer, a parallel and 25 pin serial cable, an A4 paper tray, a letter tray, and an A3 tray.

How to connect the printer

Grab the blue cable and connect it to the parallel port of your IBM compatible machine. If you decide you would like to connect the printer to the serial port in your machine, you must adjust the dip switches inside the left front panel of the laser printer as instructed on Page 4-5. Otherwise your machine is connected.

Figure 3

This is an alternative approach for a book, very popular with maintenance manuals and user documentation. The text is set on narrow width (approximately two columns out of a three-column grid). Subheads are set to the left in bold or italic typestyle for easier user reference.

PageMaker features for long publications

Particular PageMaker features which are important for working with long publications include:

Templates. Once set up, these allow a total consistency of document layout from chapter to chapter. The paragraph style sheet capability allows chapter headers, subheads or body text to be quickly changed or modified throughout the entire publication.

Convenient Text Editing. PageMaker's text editing function allows for rapid correction of text. Font or style changes can be easily performed.

Master Pages. This embraces the concept of automatic column guides, automatic headers and footers, and automatic page and chapter numbering. Repeating of constant text and graphic objects on multiple pages are also possible through the master pages.

Chapter 15 Exercise
Guidelines for Books, Manuals, and
User Documentation

In this exercise we reinforce some of the PageMaker features that lend themselves to long document creation, but most importantly we highlight some of the problems you may come up against and look at ways to solve them.

1. Create a new Pagemaker document and set your pages up with the following specifications (see Figures 4 and 5):

(i) B5 page size

(ii) Margins of 1.0 inch all around

(iii) Double-sided and Facing pages

(iii) One column

Save your new document as MY ARTICLE (Macintosh user or an abbreviated version for a PC user).

```
Page setup                              [  OK  ]

Page size:  ○ Letter    ○ Legal    ○ Tabloid   [Cancel]
            ○ A4   ○ A3   ○ A5   ◉ B5
            ○ Custom: [6.929]  by [9.842]   inches

Orientation:  ◉ Tall  ○ Wide

Start page #: [1]      # of pages:  1            ▶

Options:  ☒ Double-sided  ☒ Facing pages

Margin in inches:   Inside  [1      ]    Outside [1]
                    Top  [1]    Bottom  [1]
```

Figure 4.

Set the page size to B5, a typical size for many books and documentation (Page setup commmand from the File menu).

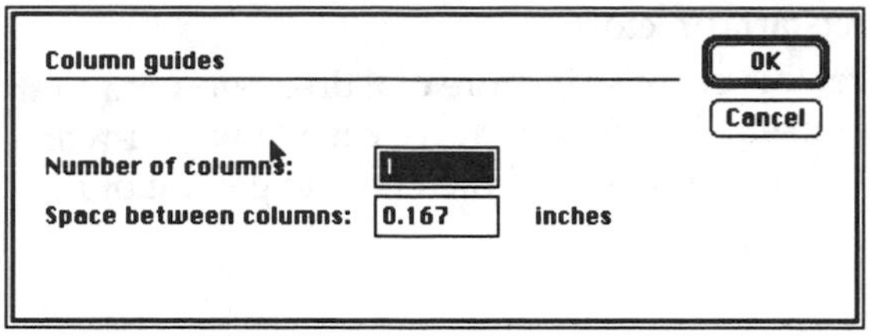

Column guides

OK

Cancel

Number of columns: [1]

Space between columns: [0.167]   inches

Figure 5.
Make sure the page is set up with one column under the Column guides command, Option menu.

On the first page, type in the following paragraphs:

Tech Tile joins the Desktop Publishing Revolution
By Fred and Mary Bloggs
Copyright © 1988 Fred Bloggs
Published By Desktop Training Systems
ISBN: 7-4563-2343-4764-48953-1234

Dedicated to Simone, without whose help this book would not have been possible.

 File Edit Options Page Type Lines Shades

Camera

Toolbox

Tech Tile joins the Desktop Publishing Revolution
By Fred and Mary Bloggs
Copyright © 1988 Fred Bloggs
Published By Desktop Training Systems
ISBN: 7-4563-2343-4764-48953-1234

Dedicated to Simone, without whose help this book would not have been possible

L R

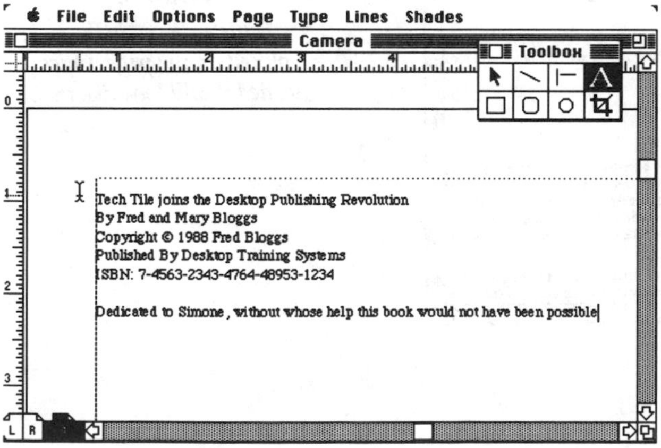

Figure 6.
Type in these paragraphs onto the first page.

2. Insert two new pages and place the text file *Bulletin Text*, found in the Getting Started folder (Figures 7 and 8), into pages 2 and 3. PageMaker PC users would place Bulletin.Doc from the Getstart directory.

From here, this exercise is more of a do-as-you-read rather than doing it yourself. This is so that we can show you when you are likely to run into trouble, and then how to get out of it.

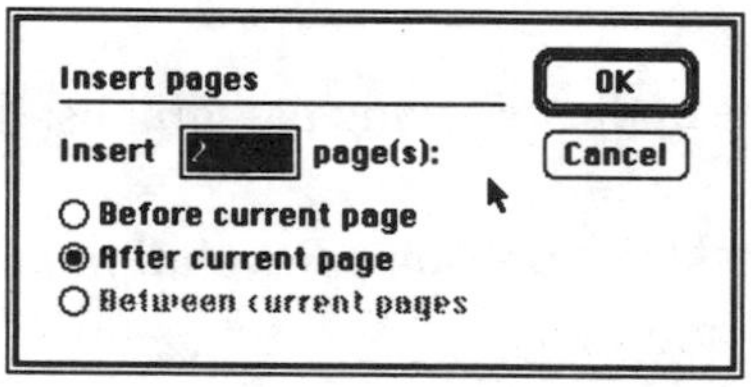

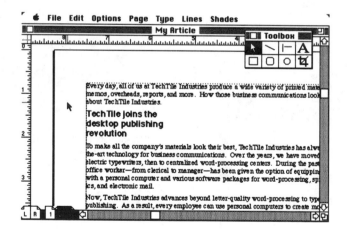

Figure 7.
Two new pages must be inserted using the Insert pages command under the pages menu.

Figure 8.
Bulletin Text is then placed on the page. Once loaded it will look like this.

3. Set Body Text font, type size, and leading.

The first thing we are going to do is select *Define Styles* Command under the **Type** menu. Highlight the *Body text* option and select the *Edit* command. This is so we can then modify the font, type size, and leading. For this, we want an extremely readable face, a serif typeface. If Times is the only font available for you to use, then select it, although another face like Palatino or New Century Schoolbook could also be suitable.

The size must also be a good readable size, around 10-12 point. This again is a personal choice.

Type specifications			OK
Font: Palatino			Cancel
Size: 11 ▷ points	Leading: 13 ▷ points		
Case: Normal	Position: Normal		

Type style:
☒ Normal ☐ Italic ☐ Underline ☐ Shadow
☐ Bold   ☐ Outline ☐ Strikethru ☐ Reverse

Figure 9.
Type size could be anywhere between 9-12 point. 11 point is probably the optimum size, but 12 point is still good.

The leading (line-spacing) for the Body text should be around 10 to 20 percent greater than the size of the type. The best for 9 point text is 11 point leading; for 10 point type, either 11 or 12 point; for 11 point type, either 12 or 13 point leading; and for 12 point type, 13 to 14 point leading is favored. For more details and research on this topic, refer to Chapter 20.

We have chosen in Figure 9, 11 point type size on 13 point leading.

4. Set justification, indents, and paragraph spacing.

To create more readable type, the paragraph alignment should always be set to justified. From reader surveys reported on earlier in this book, reader comprehension is increased when text is justified.

Each paragraph can also use a first line indent of around 0.1 to 0.2 inch, as this enables readers to more easily locate individual paragraphs.

Set the *Alignment* of Body Text to justified, and adjust the line indent to read 0.15 inch. To make sure that the text line is not too wide, set the *Left indent* for Body Text to 1 inch. The text will now be around 50–60 characters in width.

```
┌─────────────────────────────────────────────┐
│ Paragraph specifications           ( OK )    │
│ Hyphenation: ☒ Auto  ☐ Prompted    (Cancel)  │
│ Pair kerning: ☒ Auto above [12]  points      │
│ Alignment: ○ Left  ○ Right  ○ Center  ⦿ Justify │
│ Indents:              Spacing:               │
│   Left: [1]    inches   Before: [0]   inches │
│   First: [.15] inches   After:  [0]   inches │
│   Right: [0]   inches                        │
└─────────────────────────────────────────────┘
```

Figure 10.
Always justify Body text when the copy is long, and it is also a good idea to give the Body text a first line indent and a small amount of space after.

Once you have completed your editing of the Body Text style sheet, select all text on pages 2 and 3 by inserting the text tool any where within the text on the second page and typing Command–A /Ctrl A. Under the **Options** menu select the *Style palette* option. When the Style palette appears on screen select the new modified Body Text style, and the whole article will then change its appearance. When the Style palette is not required, just click in the small box in the top left-hand corner and it will disappear.

6. Set first page Styles

Move back to the first page of the article, where we typed in the initial paragraphs. We are now going to modify the appearance of the initial paragraphs. The traditional book is, however, going to use very few modifications.

The name of the article, to appear on the inside cover or somewhere nearby, is the first style we are going to edit.

Generally, the typeface will be the same typeface as the Body Text. We will bold the first paragraph, and change its point size to 24 and justification to centered. Make sure the leading is auto. Because there is only one title page, there is no need to create a style sheet for each paragraph.

7. The next paragraph is identical, but we could change the point size to 18 point. This is the paragraph, "By Fred and Mary Bloggs."

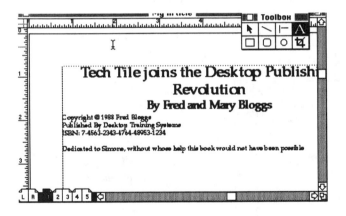

Figure 11.
This is how your Title page should look after you have changed the attributes of the titles.

8. Modify reverse page paragraphs

The information contained in the next few paragraphs (Copyright, Published By, and ISBN) is contained normally on the reverse of the title page. You will need to insert two new pages after page 1. The attributes for copyright apply to the two paragraphs following, except for the spacing above.

The font of the Copyright paragraph will be 10 point italic (the typeface should remain as it was). About 2 inches of space should be added before this paragraph to move it down from the top of the page a bit, and center it. With the pointer tool and scroll bars, move this to page 2. You may need to hit the Return key in order for the spacing of 2 inches appear.

9. Set dedication page

The final paragraph that we typed, the dedication, will also have its own attributes. The dedication will also appear on a page of its own, about halfway down the page (Figure 14). Consequently, it will have to be altered as such:

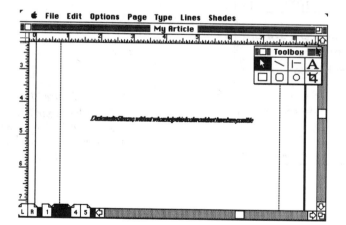

Figure 12.
The dedication is now on its own on Page 3.

Change its font to italics, its alignment centered.
Set the spacing before to 3.5 inches.

10. Create a blank page

In order for the first page of our article to begin on a right-hand page, as it should, we are going to have to create a blank page, because at the moment it would start on a left-hand page. Create a blank page by moving to page 3 (the dedication page) and select *Insert Pages* command in the **Page** menu.

11. Set other style sheets

We will now create the few style sheets that are going to be used in conjunction with Body Text throughout the article. To do this, move to the start of the story itself on page 5.

Edit styles as you like for the subheadings and the bullet paragraphs (Figure 15). However, there are a few things you might set to make the process a little easier:

Set the subheads off to the left, so that they are easily found.

Bold all headings, but keep them in the same typeface.

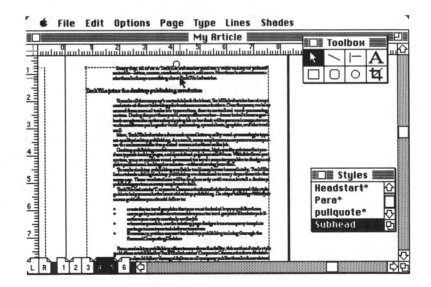

Figure 13.
A reduced view of our Page 5 after we have created and applied some of our style sheet tags.

Large files

It is unfortunate that no really large files are provided with PageMaker so that you could see the difference that is made when working with large files. The largest PageMaker provided file is only a few pages long, so it is a little hard to actually make this a long document. However, here are a few points to remember about large text files:

The largest single text file that can be loaded into PageMaker is 300K to 500K, depending on the format it was created in.

When loading files that are as large as this, be prepared to wait a few minutes, depending on the speed of your machine. Page-Maker loads the text file into memory, hyphenating the text file as it goes.

Because PageMaker, when chapters are reopened, rehyphenates all text again, large PageMaker chapters may take several minutes to open.

Be prepared, also, for a decrease in performance from your Macintosh when handling very large files.

The largest PageMaker document you can create is 128 pages. You must have multiple files for larger documents.

Save your work regularly, as you may end up loosing some if there is a crash.

12. Set headers

The next thing we are going to add to our books are the headers and footers.

Go to Master Pages and set up the headers so that the outside top of the header reads "Tech Tile," and the inside top reads "Page 1." After typing "Page" anywhere in the space, then type Command-Option-P to set up automatic page numbering. Do the same for the Right Master page, making sure you place this in the correct position with the text tool. (Figure 15).

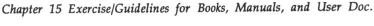

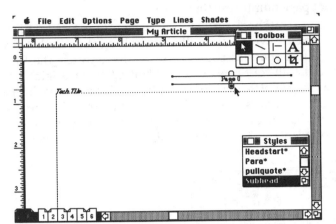

Figure 14.
*Set up the headers as shown
in the diagram.*

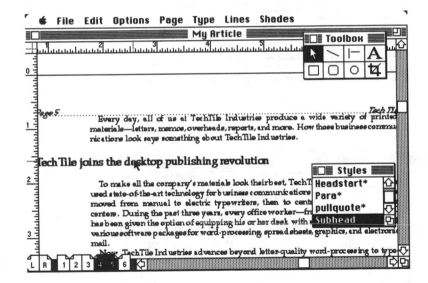

Figure 15.
*A successful header will look like this. The header itself will probably need a little adjusting,
because it may take on the appearance of body text, including the indents the body text uses.
This header has also been italicized.*

13. Set page numbering (in detail)

Page one of our book really begins where "Our Article" file was first loaded in—which is actually physical page five. So that physical page five starts as page 1, we will have to use the *Save as* command. Call your new document "Intro." In the original document we must delete the first four introduction pages so that page 1 appears on our first page. In Intro we have to delete pages 5 and 6, then go back to our master pages and delete the two headers, as we don't want them to appear in this section of the article.

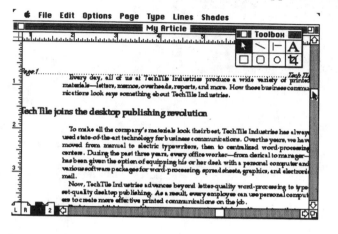

Figure 16.
Page 1 should look like this.

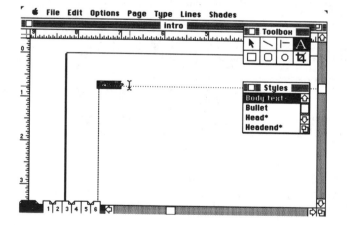

Figure 17.
Go to master pages and delete all items on it.

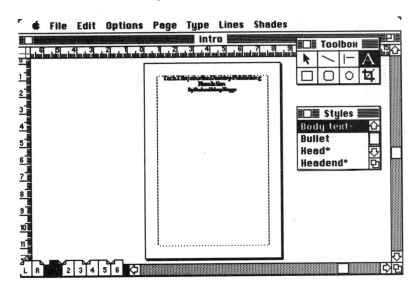

Figure 18.
How page 1 of Intro should look.

This exercise may have been a little hypothetical, but it does serve to show the ability of PageMaker, particularly for long documentation creation.

Chapter 16
Principles of Modern Design

Chapter 16
Principles of Modern Design

In this chapter we step away from conventional design, and take a look at what is known as *modern* design, although the principles have been around for more than sixty years.

Modern design is not the result of new principles of design or composition. It is the result of new methods of applying the basic conventions that have been used for decades.

Balance, tone, harmony, and proportion are principles that never change. It's the way in which these principles are interpreted that makes the arrangements different or modern.

A simple example is the placing of one word on a page. In conventional design, the word should be placed about three-eighths down the page, in what we call the focal point.

In modern design, to allow motion, the word can be placed towards the right of the page near the top or the bottom. This enables the eye to read the word quickly as it enters the page at the top, or leaves it at the bottom.

By positioning the word at the right, it can also double as a pointing device, indicating that there is more to come on the next page.

The fundamental difference between traditional and modern design principles is that one is passive and one is active, although not necessarily aggressive. In fact, it is when design becomes aggressive that the typography overpowers the message and therefore fails.

Assymetry and contrast are some of the tools of modern typography.

Basic principles

The traditional method of positioning type masses on both sides of a center axis are avoided in modern typography.

A common feature of modern design is to arrange type masses on either side of a vertical axis, that is, to the right or left of the actual vertical center axis.

In modern design, only simple easy-to-read type designs should be used. Modernizing demands simplicity. Type designs (fonts), as well as the borders and ornaments, are generally free from extravagant decoration.

Modern layouts generally give the reader the feeling of straight, stiff, yet simple design. The type selected should reflect this. Sans serif typefaces are in, as are square or straight serif faces such as modern Roman. Old style Roman faces with curved serifs are out.

To give contrast in modern design, script and types can be used, but with great care as they can be hard to comprehend.

Figure 1 illustrates these points.

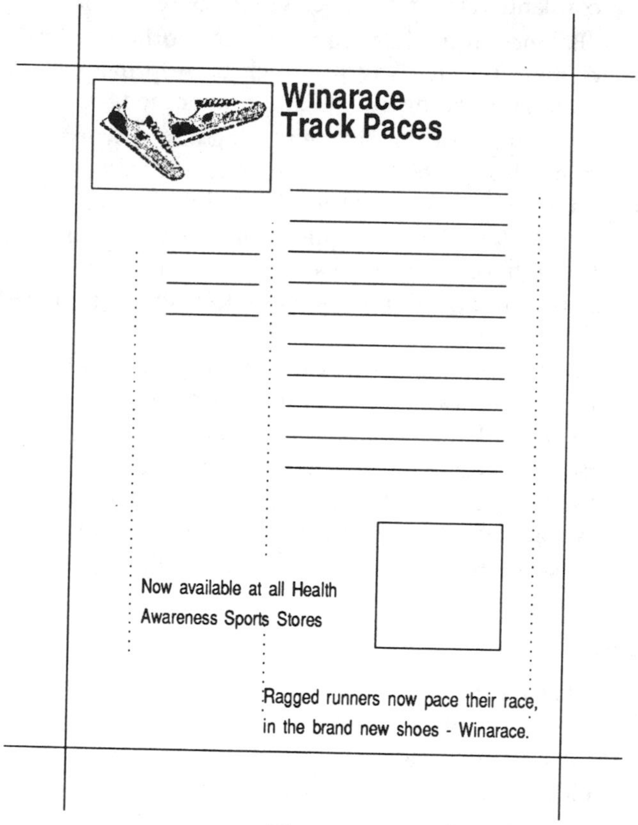

Winarace Track Paces

Now available at all Health Awareness Sports Stores

Ragged runners now pace their race, in the brand new shoes - Winarace.

Figure 1.
Examples of modern design.

Movement

Much of the rationale behind modern design is about motion, which is why modern layout has great influence in advertising design.

Illustrations and rules can easily create a sense of movement in a design. Rules can also be used in modern design to direct the eye through a layout, as a rule is a dot or point in motion.

Vertical rules are used to bring the eye from one group of type to another. If you have one group of type high on the page, in the focal area, and another towards the bottom, in the fringe, the white space in the center may drive the reader away. However, if a rule is placed between the two type groups, the reader is led through the white area to the second group of type.

By the same token, horizontal rules can help the reader to travel across the page or on to the succeeding page.

A combination of horizontal and vertical rules can direct the reader across, down, and out of the page.

Also in modern design the conventional use of margins is not employed. Only type is constrained to the central section of the page. Rules, illustrations and areas of tint are allowed to run free to the edges of the page. This is called *bleeding*. Even here there are rules. Not every illustration can be allowed to run to the edge of the page. A good rule is to bleed only those pictures which have some motion inherent in them, or a feeling of space. There are instances also when color rules across the opening of a folded newsletter could be bled.

Headline groups

In modern design, squared or staggered headline groups may be used, and grouped flush left or flush right.

Always remember, in any design, that each element or grouping must relate to another on the page to ensure balance and harmony.

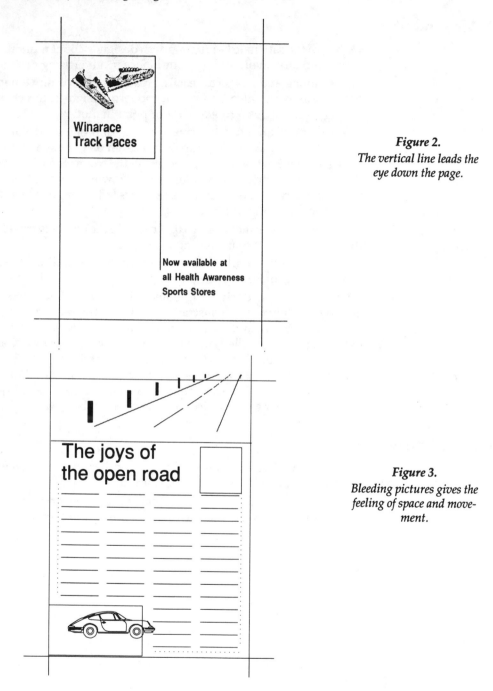

**Winarace
Track Paces**

Now available at
all Health Awareness
Sports Stores

Figure 2.
The vertical line leads the
eye down the page.

The joys of
the open road

Figure 3.
Bleeding pictures gives the
feeling of space and move-
ment.

Ornamentation

Borders, decorations, and enhancements must be in tune with modern design. Simplicity is the key. Flowery borders and busy decorations should not be used in modern design.

The most popular style of decoration in modern design is squares, circles, triangles, and stars. These geometric spots can be used advantageously—if they have a purpose. Don't go berserk with geometric shapes and colors. It is a waste of space and distracting to the reader.

Before adding ornamentation of any kind, always analyze if it really helps convey the intended message. Make your decision on the outcome accordingly.

Freedom

Modern design allows considerable freedom, which should be taken advantage of while not forgetting the parameters of good sense and comprehensibility.

There are, however, a number of design devices which should be treated warily. These include:

- Placing the design on an angle to create added motion and attract attention. This can be effective, if the intention is to have your design singled out from others in a page of advertising.
- If the design is interesting, the reader may not notice or be bothered with the angle of the text. Be careful not to tilt the text too much—the reader is easily put off.
- Running type lines up the edge of the page or around corners must be handled very carefully. The vertical type line works only if the material used is inconsequential, such as a slogan. For example, it can be quite effective on menus, with the name of the establishment running down the edge of the page. The general thinking in this instance, is that the diners are already in the establishment when they see the menu.

Chapter 17
Printing in Color

Chapter 17
Printing in Color

Any color as long as it's black

Consider this page. It looks very much like any other page, with its ordinary black type printed on ordinary white paper.

Color the type blue, and see how much more attractive the page becomes to the reader's eye. If you were to show potential readers the two pages together, the chances are that eight out of ten would find the blue printed page more attractive than the black one, and that nine out of ten would probably describe the black page as boring.

But ask those people now to read the two pages, and we're in a different ball game.

The chances, now, are that seven out of ten who read the black text, would display comprehension sound enough to enable them to digest the text and act on any message it contains. Of those who attempt to read the visually more attractive colored text, only one out of ten will display good comprehension.

Not a very attractive result, you may agree, particularly if the aim of the text is to sell something.

Spot color can do wonders for advertising revenue. US research tells us about one advertiser, who paid a loading of 70 percent for spot color, and drew nearly 400 percent more sales. Spot color generally adds to the cost of an advertisement by 20 percent or more, but the advertisement is noted by 63 percent more people and results in 64 percent more sales.

Some negative reaction may occur with single spot color advertisements in full-color magazines. In some cases this has drawn a lower than expected response. The thinking is that the client could not afford full color.

What the research doesn't tell us is how the color was used. One can understand a positive impact when spot color is used on logotypes and ideograms such as BP, Shell, Ford, the Mitsubishi diamonds, Coke and so on, but what about headlines? Or the text?

What's the effect on the reader if the color is used as part or all of the message, instead of as an ancillary?

Color imparts a feeling of excitement, and most certainly is a magnet for the eyes.

The purpose of the tests reported below was to determine whether, at the same time, color used in headlines or text might impede comprehension.

Colored headlines

Most frequent use of color in headlines is *high chroma* color, such as a mixture of the *process* colors, cyan and magenta.

Other high chroma colors, such as hot red, bright green, and orange, are becoming more and more common in newspaper and magazines, as run of press color availability increases.

Tests were made of both high chroma and low chroma colors.

In the first tests, colors used were magenta (process red), cyan (process blue), hot red (100 parts magenta, 100 yellow), hot orange (100 yellow, 40 magenta), and lime green (100 yellow, 40 cyan).

Results applying to each individual color were so similar as to enable a general conclusion to be drawn about high chroma color in headlines.

The test procedure was identical to previous ones, with the obvious exception that color headlines were substituted for black headlines.

This aspect of the program attracted considerable comment from readers.

- 61 percent of all readers said they found high chroma colors most attractive, drawing their attention quickly to the text.

- 47 percent said they then found the headings hard to read.

- 64 percent said they found the color intruding while they were trying to read the text.

- 12 percent said they felt the same effect as an obtrusive light, or an over-bright color television picture—distracting the eyes.

- 10 percent found the high chroma colors intense and tending to cause eye tiredness.

The stock used for this series of tests was, as with all tests, non-reflective.

A small number of readers (2 percent) indicated afterwards that, anxious to continue the test to the best of their ability, they folded the pages over to mask the colored headlines, and to enable them to concentrate better. An inspection of retrieved papers showed this to be the case.

The tests for low chroma colors were done in an identical manner.

The low chroma colors chosen were deep blue (100 parts cyan, 50 black), dark emerald (100 yellow, 100 cyan, 40 black); purple (100 cyan, 100 magenta); and plum red (100 magenta, 60 black). Comments made on these tests implied that the colored headlines didn't have the same magnetic quality that the high chroma colors had.

However, there was a degree of attraction, in both positive and negative aspects. The good comprehension levels in this test were three times as high as those for high chroma colors, but less than 80 percent of those for black headings. Results follow in Table 1.

Table 1	Comprehension level		
	Good	**Fair**	**Poor**
	%	%	%
(a) Layout with black headlines	67	19	14
(b) Layout using high chroma color headlines	17	18	65
(c) Layout using low chroma color headlines	52	28	20

Obviously, there's a paradox. To be valuable as an eye catching device, a colored headline needs to be in a vibrant color, which tends to disqualify it as a means of communication.

The study showed that the darker the headline, the greater the comprehension level. This poses the question: Why not black? Ink doesn't come any darker!

Comments made by readers show that the use of process colors in headlines is dangerous. Although the results indicated greater comprehension levels than, say, layouts set in sans serif body type, the spot color headlines in high chroma showed a greater potential to antagonize some readers.

This is not a recommendation that a ban be placed on heading spot color. Used judiciously and sparingly, it can be a most compelling and useful heading feature. But great care should be taken that the color doesn't get in the way of the message.

Colored text

In the past five years, the use of colored text, and text printed on colored tints, has proliferated, without, as it were, benefit of clergy.

Little or no research exists, either to support or condemn the practice.

Miles Tinker, with his Legibility of Print (Iowa State University Press, 1963), stands almost in isolation. His view is that there should be at least a 70 percent differential between text and background—that is, if the text is printed solid, then the background should be no more than 30 percent tint.

Obviously, this might be held to apply for black, or dark colors such as deep purple, navy blue, dark brown. But what about cyan, or magenta, which are much lighter to start with? What effect does printing text in cyan on a 30 percent cyan tint have on the reader?

In an attempt to remedy this loophole in research, tests were run using text printed in black and in several colors on white paper; in black and several colors on tinted paper; in black on shades of gray; in reverse, using black and color; and in bold type, contrasted with the normal medium-density type used in advertising and newspaper editorial for body text.

For the color text studies, articles presented to the readers were set in 10 point Times Roman type over 12 picas (13 cm or 5 inches) to a depth of 46 cm (18 inches), three columns to a page. Each article had a single line heading set in 36 point Univers, Bold, lowercase, printed black, and above the three legs of text.

The layout and type employed were in a format which previous research had shown offers minimal distraction for the reader, thus enabling the text matter in its varied hues to stand or fall solely on the merits of those hues.

All results given are expressed in percentages of the total sample.

Articles were presented to readers in six forms: in black; in PMS 259, a deep purple; in PMS 286, French blue; in PMS 399, a muted color resembling olive green; and in two high-intensity colors, warm red and process blue (cyan)—all on white paper.

When the text was printed black, the comprehension levels were similar to those obtained in previous tests conducted on similarly designed material.

The good comprehension level was 70 percent; fair comprehension 19 percent; and poor comprehension 11 percent.

(There is probably nothing the typographer can do to ensure a 100 percent level of good comprehension on anything more complex than today's page of the desk calendar.)

The responses to text printed in colors showed a considerably lower level of good comprehension than in the tests for black printed on white.

Initially, tests were conducted separately on matt and gloss paper, it being considered possible that what was good on matt might be even better on gloss; or that glossy paper might, through its reflective quality, be an inferior reading medium.

However, results showed little variation in good comprehension levels. During the tests it was noticed that, when readers experienced discomfort because of reflection from glossy paper, they altered their positions, or the position of the paper, to minimize this problem.

Tests of matt versus gloss were conducted with text printed in black; in medium-intensity color, and in high-intensity color. In each instance, results were within 2 percent of each other. As this variation was statistically insignificant, the tests were abandoned, and all further tests conducted on uncoated (bond) paper.

At the conclusion of each test on colored text, participants were asked to comment on the presentation of each paper. A summary of comments:

- 76 percent said they found text printed in high-intensity colors difficult to read. The color tended to break concentration, they said, and many found they lost their place and had to recapitulate. The brightness of the color appeared to cause lines to merge, making reading difficult. There was no variation in the extremity of this effect between text set in process blue and warm red.

- An analysis of questions and answers showed that few readers retained any comprehension of the text printed in bright colors, beyond the first few paragraphs.

- 41 percent of readers indicated there was insufficient contrast between brightly colored text and the paper background, despite the intensity of the color.

- 68 percent indicated the same effect when the text was printed in olive green (PMS 399).

- On being shown pages printed in black and in cyan, 90 percent said they found the black page boring when compared with the blue printed page.

- And 81 percent said they would prefer to read the colored page because it was more attractive. The consequences of accepting this view follow in Table 2.

- 63 percent said the medium intensity color, PMS 286, provided concentration problems. Again, lines of type appeared to merge. This phenomenon occurred less with the low intensity color (deep purple), and hardly at all with black.

- All of those (36 percent of the sample), who exhibited poor comprehension of the text printed deep purple, said they believed their concentration suffered simply because they were aware the text wasn't printed black.

- *Every* reader said he or she would prefer to read text printed in black.

Results of the comprehension tests are shown in Table 2.

Table 2	Comprehension level		
	Good	**Fair**	**Poor**
	%	%	%
Text printed in black	70	19	11
Low-intensity color (PMS 259) deep purple	51	13	36
Medium-intensity color (PMS 286) French blue	29	22	49
Muted color (PMS 399) olive green	10	13	77
High-intensity color cyan or warm red	10	9	81

Text on tinted ground

The second series of tests was conducted, using identical methodology, into the comprehensibility of text printed on tinted backgrounds.

Six separate series of tests were conducted, using black on process blue tints; PMS 259 (deep purple) on its tints; PMS 286 (French blue) on its tints; process blue on its tints; black on tints of olive green (PMS 399) and PMS 399 on its tints.

Readers were given samples, with text printed on tints of 10 percent of the base color, and increased in strength in increments of 10 percent.

Again, readers were invited to comment on the presentation of the text. More than half of those who responded to the invitation made a comment with an interesting marketing application: at low-strength tint, the tint seemed to soften the harshness of the white paper (this supposed harshness had not been mentioned before, nor was afterwards). The softening effect of the tinted background, they said, made reading easier. At higher strength, the tint intruded and made reading more difficult.

However, while results of the test supported the latter view, they did not confirm the former.

Results of the tint tests are shown in Tables 3 to 8.

Table 3		Comprehension level		
		Good	**Fair**	**Poor**
		%	%	%
Black on cyan tint	10%	68	24	8
	20%	56	21	23
	30%	38	19	43
	40%	22	12	66

This test was discontinued when the combined results for good and fair comprehension failed to reach 50 percent of the total.

Table 4		Comprehension level		
		Good	**Fair**	**Poor**
		%	%	%
PMS 259 on tint	10%	50	14	36
	20%	32	10	58
Table 5				
PMS 286 on tint	10%	27	16	57
	20%	12	10	78
Table 6				
Cyan on cyan tint	10%	6	7	87
	20%	nil	2	98
Table 7				
Black on PMS 299 tint	10%	68	26	6
	20%	53	21	26
	30%	32	19	49
	40%	22	13	65

This test was discontinued when the combined results for good and fair comprehension failed to reach 50 percent of the total.

Table 8		Comprehension level		
		Good	Fair	Poor
		%	%	%
PMS 399 on PMS 399 tint	10%	8	8	84
	20%	2	6	92
	30%	0	3	97

In these tests of lighter or more intense color on tints, participants displayed their strongest reactions to any aspect of the program.

In the test of cyan on a 10 percent tint of cyan, 42 percent of readers indicated they had not attempted to continue reading seriously after a few paragraphs.

When the tint was increased to 20 percent, the percentage of "conscientious objectors" rose to 53 percent.

This declared stance was supported by an analysis of the results. For example, in the tests with cyan on a 20 percent cyan tint, 99 percent of correct answers related to questions in the first leg of text, indicating a reluctance or inability to digest the entire article. Yet the same articles, presented in black to control groups, offered no difficulties.

The reasons given by the readers included the apparent brightness of the color, and the difficulty readers had in distinguishing text from background. The brightness element applied also during tests using PMS 286.

The same results were apparent in the test of PMS 399 on tints of the same color, but brightness wasn't a problem with this test. The principle reason given was the similarity in color of text and background.

Readers said they found the test using PMS 259 on its 10 percent tint pleasant to the eyes, but many said they were conscious of the presence of color, which may have affected concentration.

Prior to the tests, readers were shown, simultaneously, printed pages in all three forms (black on white, black on tint, and color on tint) and asked to make subjective judgements on their relative attractiveness.

Results of this test contrasted markedly with those of an earlier experiment into the relative attractiveness of black and colored text, discussed previously.

Table 9 shows the results of this test:

Table 9	Most attractive
	%
Black text	8
Black on 10 percent cyan	88
Cyan on 10 percent cyan	4
Black text	17
Black on 10 percent olive green	83
Olive green on 10 percent olive green	0

From this assessment, it would appear that black text printed on light tint is an attractive marketing proposition, as well as having high comprehensibility.

It would also appear that not only are colors on their tints extremely difficult to comprehend; they are also unattractive to the reader, except when the color is of low intensity and dark.

There is obviously a cost factor in printing a second color. But to judge by the readers' assessments, and the objective comprehension levels recorded in this study, there must also be a considerable marketing benefit in printing black on a tint.

By the same criteria, there must also be a considerable cost disadvantage in printing in one color—if that color is not black.

Black on not so black

A frequently used variation on the use of black on tinted grounds is to print black text on shades of gray.

This is generally used when only one color is available, in an attempt to present associated material in manner different from that used for the main text.

The same methodology was used to test the comprehensibility of this element, and the results are shown in Table 10.

Table 10	Comprehension level		
	Good	Fair	Poor
	%	%	%
Black on white	70	19	11
Black on 10% black	63	22	15
Black on 20% black	33	18	49
Black on 30% black	3	10	87

This test was discontinued when the combined results for good and fair comprehension failed to reach 50 percent of the total.

One significant comment, made frequently as the shade strength increased beyond 10 percent, was that readers were experiencing more difficulty discerning the words—like trying to read a newspaper in a poor light.

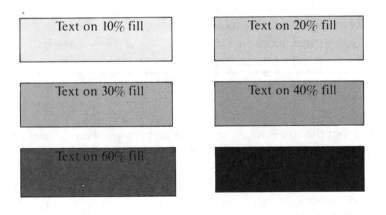

Figure 1.
Examples of black text on tinted gray background.

Into reverse

David Ogilvy says that advertising copy should never be set in reverse, nor over gray or colored tint. He says that the old school "believed these devices forced people to read the copy; we now know that they make reading physically impossible."

The results of tests of text in black on light color tints oppose his view; the tests on black text set on shades of gray are more on his side; and three tests on text printed in reverse on black or dark colors support his view.

Comments made on the completion of the reverse tests were that a form of light vibration, similar to, but worse than, that encountered when text was printed in high-intensity colors, seemed to make the lines of type move and merge into one another.

Eighty percent of the sample reported this phenomenon.

Results are shown in Table 11.

Table 11	Comprehension level		
	Good	Fair	Poor
	%	%	%
Text printed black on white	70	19	11
Text printed white on black	0	12	88
Text printed white on PMS259	2	16	82
Text printed white on PMS286	0	4	96

There is a school of thought which agrees that reversing can be fraught with danger, but only if serif type is used. The argument is that the fine strokes and serifs disappear when the material is reversed. (Type size is also important.)

To test this, similar articles were prepared set in 10 point Univers, with all other dimensions being identical to the remainder of the test papers.

With the text printed black, comprehension levels were comparable with those recorded in the texts of sans serif verus serif body matter.

Good comprehension was 14 percent, fair comprehension 25 percent, and poor comprehension 61 percent. With the text reversed, comprehensibility dropped considerably.

Good comprehension dropped to 4 percent, and fair comprehension to 13 percent. Poor comprehension rose to 83 percent.

It could be said that the depreciation in comprehensibility appears to be proportionately less when the type is set in sans serif—but this argument only holds water if a level of good comprehension of less than 5 percent is considered acceptable.

David Ogilvy says that advertising copy should never be set in reverse, nor over gray or colored tint. He says that the old school "believed these devices forced people to read the copy; we now know that they make reading physically impossible."

The results of tests of text in black-on light color tints oppose his view; the tests on black text set on shades of gray are more on his side; and three tests on text printed in reverse on black or dark colors support his view.

Comments made on the completion of the reverse tests were that a form of light vibration, similar to, but worse than, that encountered when text was printed in high-intensity colors, seemed to make the lines of type move and merge into one another.

Eighty percent of the sample reported this phenomenon.

Results are shown in Table 11.

Figure 2.
Example of body text from the previous page set in reverse.

Bold and bad

A final series of tests was conducted with text printed in bold type. This generally is used as a means of separating a subsidiary article from a major one, or to break up the monotony of an article.

It certainly has those effects. It also has the effect of ensuring that the subsidiary article is harder to read. Readers in this test complained of fatigue, similar to that experienced when text was printed in high- or medium-intensity colors.

The bold text, occupying more of the letter space allocated to it than normal Roman type, seemed to some readers to be cramped.

To others it seemed to set up a halo effect, carrying the outline of letters into adjoining letters and on to the lines above and below. Results are shown below in Table 12.

Table 12	Comprehension level		
	Good	Fair	Poor
	%	%	%
Text printed in Times Roman	70	19	11
Text printed in Times Bold	30	20	50

Conclusion

It's impossible to avoid the fact that comprehensibility of colored text increases as the color gets closer to black.

So why not use black, and employ color where it's best suited, as a complement to the message?

We should consider carefully Edmund Arnold's advice: "Start with good typography—the kind that best suits the reader—and use color to reinforce the communication."

The best colors to use

When using colors for printed material, there are a few things to consider. Is the cost worth the result? What is the best color to use? If using more than one color, which ones harmonize the best?

There are three types of color harmony:

1. Monochromatic harmony

This is achieved by using two or more tones of the same color. If one base color is used, harmony will always result.

2. Analogous harmony

Close primary and secondary colors are harmonic. That is, yellow harmonizes with green; green with blue, blue with violet, and so on. This is because there is a common factor in each harmony. Green is made up of yellow and blue, so it harmonizes with both.

3. Complementary harmony

Colors directly opposite one another are complementary. Yellow harmonizes with violet; orange with blue, red with green. Adjacent colors also harmonize, red and green for example, but this is also dependent on saturation and hue.

Chapter 18
Guidelines for Advertisements

Chapter 18
Guidelines for Advertisements

Elements of design

Producing and exhibiting a piece of marketing literature or an advertisement is an expensive business. Keeping this always in mind, we must ensure that our message is as efficient as possible.

Keep in mind also that a design has to:

- *Attract attention*

- *Create interest*

- *Create desire*

- *Tell how that desire might be satisfied*

The designer does all of this by the way the elements of the design are placed on the page.

There are four basic elements:

- *Illustration*

- *Headline*

- *Text*

- *Address details of the advertiser*

Using these four points, a method must be devised of placing them so that the four take effect in sequence.

We start with thumbnail sketches. These can be used to place the elements in position.

If the picture is interesting, it could well be the element that attracts the attention. Or it could be a fairly dull picture, used only to support the words. In that instance, the headline could well become the feature that attracts attention and creates interest.

If you have several headlines, you should select the one that has the greatest impact on the message. *Never lose sight of the aim of the piece you're designing and who it is aimed at.*

Keep in mind also, the earlier chapter on reading patterns; left to right, top to bottom. After thousands of years we still read that way.

The attention attracting device should be placed at or near the top of the page, with the device extended to create interest. The text should also follow on in a logical sequence to give the reader more relevant information.

Do not make the reader work hard for the information. Make it as easy as you can for them to find, read, and understand your message. Keep it simple.

After giving the message and relevant information, you may want to tell the reader where he/she can obtain this product or service. This can often be quite effectively achieved by use of a small corporate logo, along with the address and telephone information. This also adds to corporate identity, when advertising or publishing for the general public, possibly in an outside medium.

Corporate identity is a very useful marketing tool. To be truly effective, it is essential for the use of the identity to be consistent with the presentation and design.

Examples of good and bad advertisements follow.

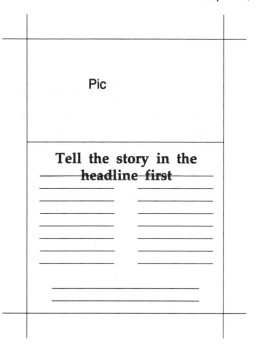

This is an acceptable advertisement. The following rules have been obeyed:

1. Attract attention by placing the attention-grabbing illustration at the top.
2. Tell the story of what you are selling in the headline. Few of your readers will go any further.
3. Make the text straightforward and easy to read—serif type, lowercase, justified, and black on white.
4. Tell the reader where he can buy the product by giving the name and address clearly. If there is a recognizable logo, use it, but only if it will help the sale. If the logo immediately tells the reader who is advertising (Shell, IBM, Coke), good. If not, leave it for the corporate letterhead.
5. Keep the paragraphs short. They are easier to read than long ones.

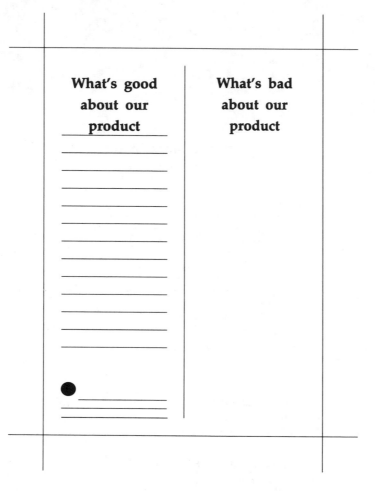

This is an acceptable advertisement. The following rules have been obeyed:

1. It's easy to follow—no barriers to jump over.
2. Lowercase headings and text for greater legibility.
3. The text flows in the normal reading manner.
4. Size of headings and text are compatible in that the reader is not forced to make two focuses to read both.

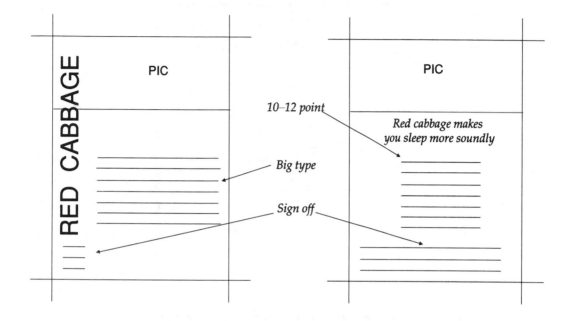

Consider the above advertisements in the light of the following comments:

1. Make sure your headline contains a message. Label headlines do not sell. They may be recalled, but that doesn't mean sales.
2. Let the headline be clear, and don't fall to the temptation to be clever. Headlines running vertically annoy readers, research shows.
3. Keep the text to a comfortable width (40–60 characters), and a comfortable size, between 10 and 12 point.
4. Use white space as a frame. If it's enclosed, it tends to explode a layout by separating items.
5. Be sure the reader is in no doubt who is advertising, or where it can be bought. Make the sign-off clear and important.

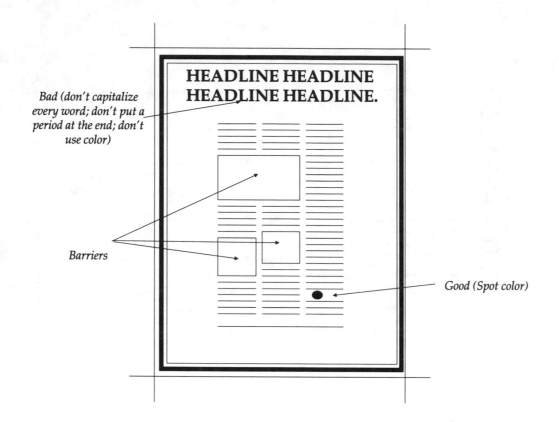

Bad (don't capitalize every word; don't put a period at the end; don't use color)

Barriers

Good (Spot color)

The above is not very acceptable for the following reasons:

1. If you use a border, be sure that it will not overpower the headline or text. If the border is noticeable, it's too big.
2. Don't capitalize every word in a headline. It slows the reader, and he'll lose interest.
3. Don't use a period at the end of the headline. it reduces the level of comprehension by suggesting the message is over. Newspapers don't.
4. Don't force the reader to jump over barriers, or confuse him/her by using them, and creating a dichotomy.
5. Use spot color sparingly. The logo, or some display element is visually enough. Color on text turns readers off, and colored headlines can affect comprehension of the following text.

The above is not acceptable for the following reasons:
1. Don't have headlines so big you force the reader to focus twice—once on the headline, and once on text.
2. Long headlines should not be set in capitals.
3. Don't kern headlines excessively.
4. Text should not be set in clever shapes—they're hard to read.
5. Don't make your coupons in unusual shapes—someone has to collate and sort them.

This is not acceptable for the following reasons:

1. Don't superimpose the headline onto the photograph. It visually becomes hard to read, and it ruins the effect of the photo by dividing attention.
2. Type should not be set at an angle for effect. You'll annoy the reader if the angle is such that the reader has to slant the page.
3. Don't reverse body text. Research shows that comprehension of reversed text is practically nil, and other research shows far better results are gained from black on white.
4. Don't set text in lines longer than sixty characters.

Chapter 19
Dealing with Printers

Chapter 19
Dealing with Printers

So, you've created your master copy of your publication in Page-Maker—now you want to have it professionally printed. This chapter will enable you to deal more effectively with printers and keep control of the project from start to finish.

Understanding the jargon

Let us first give you a rundown on some of the jargon printers commonly use—which, if learned, will help you communicate more effectively with them.

JOB - Printers refer to your newsletter, stationery, or annual report as the job they are currently working on for you.

MECHANICALS - Refers to the laser-printed or typeset masters you have supplied for printing. Often referred to in some countries as art work.

SCREENED BROMIDES - These are specially photographed images of your black and white or color original photographs. To enable clear print reproduction, a dotted image is required. Most printers can screen your original photographs.

LINE BROMIDES - This refers to a clear black and white image of a logo, line drawing, or something else, with clear black and white contrast, with no shades of gray.

CROPPING - This eliminates areas of diagrams, pictures, or art work that are not needed. Scanned images can be cropped in PageMaker. If you don't have a scanner, you must clearly mark on the back of the photograph which section you want in your publication. The alternative is to photocopy the photograph or image, and mark using a ruler and red pen the area required for printing.

TO FIT - This may be used to indicate that you want the picture or logo sized to fit the hole you have left on the master copy. Quite often this can be over more than one column.

DROP IN - This indicates that you have supplied the master copy, but the printer is still required to drop something in to a hole you have left; for example, a screened bromide of a photograph or a logo.

STRIP IN - Similar to drop in, except it relates to text rather than images. For example, the printer could strip in the change of address on the existing artwork for the business cards he holds.

FILM - If your job is complex, color, photographs, or needed in large quantities, chances are it doesn't go straight to the printing press. It is sent (sometimes to an outside specialist) for film to be made. This is handy to know if you like to get progress reports on your print job. Film is the first stage after dropping or stripping in any bits.

PLATE MAKING - The next stage after film. Metal plates are made from the supplied mechanicals (or art work) ready for printing. (Paper plates do not require film.)

SPOT COLOR - This refers to one color plus your basic black. For example, a company logo may be in spot color throughout a document. Sometimes you may have two spot colors plus your basic black.

FULL COLOR - This is when you want exact reproduction of a color photograph in all its glory. Full color is quite expensive.

PMS NUMBER - This is an international color convention that specifies the number of a specially mixed color. If you use a special mix for your corporate color, say PMS235, write it down somewhere to make sure you get the exact same color each time. However, even a PMS color may look different on a matt stock to a glossy stock.

STOCK - Refers to the paper you request for your print job.

GRIP - The printing press needs a border around your job for the print rollers to grip. You should not supply artwork that goes to the very edge of the page. (Most laser printers have a similar grip or margin default anyway.)

BLEEDING - Bleeding is the process where color is required to run to the very edges of the page. Bleeding is very expensive, because it has to be printed on oversize stock, and trimmed to get the bleeding effect. This is because the bleeding eliminates a grip for the printing press.

SCREEN WASH OUT - This refers to the pale dotted screen of a color over a page or section of a page. Often used in magazines, where a small story on a page will have a pale color behind it. This is achieved by a percentage screen of a base color, usually no more than 10 or 15%. This depends on the intensity of the base color, and it is usually best to let the printer advise on the right percentage screen.

DUMMY - You should make and send a dummy every time you request a print job from your printer. This is usually a photocopy of your master with all the elements in it. That is, you have marked or photocopied all the photos and line drawings required, and marked clearly where spot color and screens are meant to be. This is to avoid confusion if photographs and artwork are somehow separated. The dummy copy should be clearly marked "dummy for positionals only" so the printer knows to follow your layout and instructions.

RUNNING THE JOB - Basically means the job is on the press. In the case of spot color, depending on the sort of press used, your job may be printed or "run" for every separate color. Some printing presses can print multiple colors at once.

TURNAROUND - Refers to the time needed to finish the job from start to delivery.

SHELLS - These are pre-printed base jobs held at the printer's premises. For example, you may print a two color newsletter on expensive stock every month, at 1,000 copies a time. A more economical way is to print 10,000 shells up front in your second color (other than black) picking out your masthead, address details and one or two other color standard elements. The printer holds these, and each month, runs the black text over your shells to produce a very fast and inexpensive job. This can also knock a day or two off the turn-around time of your job. Business cards and personalized items are also quite cost efficient this way.

WASH-UP - Refers to the additional charges for spot colors. Every time a color is changed on the press, a wash-up is incurred on top of the cost of running the job through the press twice.

WET - Means that the ink hasn't dried and the next process cannot begin. Drying time varies from stock to stock, but in the case of normal bond stock, a couple of hours should lapse between printing one side of a job and the other, or between final printing and folding or stapling. Humidity is also a critical factor here.

TRIMMING - Cutting to a particular size (i.e., business cards), or, in the case of the bleed, requires trimming. This cannot be done until the job is considered dry, so it often adds half a day to your turnaround time.

INTERLEAVING - Blank paper can be placed between each sheet of your job, if it is too wet to trim, but is urgently required. This ensures against smudging. You can ask a printer to interleave, and a small charge is usually added for this service.

SCORING - If a heavy stock needs to be folded by hand, a score may be required. This is an indentation made by hand or machine to ensure a clean fold.

FOLDING - Again, time is added for this process. Some jobs can be machine folded. In addition, if folding is required, a folded copy of your dummy should be supplied, so the printers know which way to fold it, if the address has to be seen through a window-face envelope.

STITCHING - This refers to the stapling of your finished document. Again it is important for your dummy to clearly show exactly how you want your job stitched. Saddle-stitching refers to the staples in the spine, while corner-stitching refers to a corner staple.

ESTIMATE - A telephone quote prior to sighting the finished artwork. This protects printers for quoting on what seems a simple job, only to find that it bleeds or the inks have to be specially mixed.

When sending a job across to a printer, a covering note may read: "Print 3,500 March 89 newsletters on Tabloid (or A3) gloss art shells, held in stock in black ink, with two bromides and two screens dropped in as marked on dummy. Score and fold to Letter (or A4). Supply 1,000 flat and remainder folded in three to fit window face envelope."

Finding the right printers

Dealing with printers can sometimes be the biggest headache of all when preparing a publication—whether it be a flyer, newsletter, full color magazine, or annual report.

The first thing to come to grips with is that not all printers specialize in all sorts of printing. And when you find the right printers for your needs, stick to them. Nurture them, try to supply your end of the job in a way that makes it easy for them to supply theirs. Through personal experience, we have found that all the difficulties we had getting a "good" printer were mostly due to our inability to understand their needs, and to use the skills and knowledge they've taken years to obtain.

Always assume that the printer knows a lot about printing, and don't be afraid to ask their advice on a job—listen to them, they are often right.

You may say that's all well and good, but how do you find such a printer. There are hundreds of printers in every city, and none of them would stay in business if they didn't know their business. Most printers are OK, some are exceptional—you just have to know how to deal with them.

First understand that different printers are good at different jobs:

Instant Printers - Prefer simple jobs such as basic stationery and business cards; more single jobs than corporate accounts. Good at flyers, basic newsletters, handbills, and forms. Best to give them jobs that require only one or two colors printed on fairly basic stock.

Commercial Printers - These are specialists at large runs with often tricky color work. They are not fast like instant printers, but the quality can be remarkable. It is always good to "book" a job in, in advance, and get an agreement on turnaround time. That way they can order in any special stock or ink, and keep a press ready if it's super urgent and you're a good client. Great for annual reports, glossy magazines, large run corporate stationery, government forms, etc.

Automated Offset - Very specialized. They handle multiple-page, sometimes small run jobs, such as 200-page training manuals. Their binding and finishing are usually excellent. Due to the nature of their work, they also like jobs booked in advance, and usually like to send someone out to quote. A large job may take three weeks to turn around.

Consequently, you may deal with two or three different printers for all your corporate needs. Dealt with efficiently, using the tools described above, you should have them working for you, rather than the other way around. When trying a new printer, find out what other major accounts he has, even ask if you can call his existing clients for a referral. This can be important if you are taking a large account away from one printer to give to another.

Chapter 20
Brochure Design: A Case Study

Chapter 20
Brochure Design: A Case Study

NRMA Leaflets—How Many Are Read?

Executive summary

The NRMA (National Roads and Motorists' Association) is Australia's largest motoring organization. It is also involved in a wide range of insurance, including car, boat, and house. The study contained in this chapter was undertaken to determine the extent to which NRMA leaflets are read by members. It was conducted by the Publications Editor, Colin Wheildon, between November, 1985 and August, 1987.

The study, of 24 product marketing and community service leaflets, covered leaflets distributed to target audiences, and leaflets mailed directly to members, such as by bulk mail or inserted in the NRMA's magazine, *The Open Road*.

The main findings of the study were:

- At best, one in three members will read an NRMA leaflet, even when the members are in a target audience (that is, they have declared interest in the subject, and may have requested a leaflet). On average, the readership of NRMA targeted leaflets is one in four; at worst, one in twelve (Figure 1).

  Very little difference was recorded between readership of marketing and community service leaflets.

  If leaflets are letter-box dropped, the extent of reading falls to an average of one in twenty, with a high of one in ten, and a low of one in 100 (Figure 2).

  The low readership of letter-box dropped leaflets prevented meaningful comparison between leaflets distributed in this manner. Therefore, all data in this study which invites comparison refers to leaflets aimed at target audiences.

- One in two readers will read the headline of a leaflet and no further, irrespective of whether the leaflet is targeted or delivered gratuitously; of the subject of the leaflet; of design features; or of length of text. There is, however, no guarantee that because a headline is read it will be understood, and the message of the leaflet comprehended.

- While the number of words in a leaflet is not a factor in its readability, the size and style of the type used, and the design of the leaflet, can have considerable bearing on the reader's willingness and ability to read and comprehend the message. Therefore, when leaflets are designed, great consideration should be given to research into readers' habits and reactions.

- The most preferred type size for leaflets was 11 point on a 13 point body (Figure 3).

Figure 1. Leaflets distributed to members on request (target audience).

Leaflet title	Read by (percentage)	Headline only read	Headline understood (% of previous column)	Photography recalled	Art/ diagrams recalled
There's got to be an easier way (life bonds)	21	49	22	13	-
With the Money (Finance)	32	50	59	13	-
When it comes to... (Car)	34	45	62	23	-
Is This The End (Car)	29	42	10	-	14
Home Contents	22	44	-	10	0
Home Building	23	42	-	11	-
Home Personal Effects	19	51	100	16	-
On Site Caravan	19	42	-	-	0
Touring Caravan	20	44	-	-	0
Boatsure	21	43	84	14	-
Motor Personal Accident	32	51	-	15	-
Legal Hassles (Legal)	30	44	-	14	-
What Can You Do (Car Theft)	16	48	94	-	-
What Thieves Cost You	18	47	-	-	-
Roundabouts version 1	14	48	-	10	0
Roundabouts version 2	35	52	-	16	3
Country Roads	33	46	37	-	1
Bus Priority	20	52	-	-	4
Sorry but You're Over The Limit	34	50	100	15	-
Don't Blow It	37	62	4	-	-
How Many Drinks	8	55	-	-	-
Children Crossing	33	54	100	-	4
S. Lanes	33	54	-	-	1
Keep Left	34	51	99	-	2

- indicates not applicable or not tested

Figure 2. Leaflets distributed to members gratuitously

Leaflet title	Read by (percentage)	Headline only read	Headline understood (% of previous column)	Photography recalled	Art/ diagrams recalled
There's got to be an easier way (life bonds)	2	44	20	10	-
With the Money (Finance)	6	47	56	10	-
When it comes to... (Car)	8	47	57	10	-
Is This The End (Car)	6	52	7	-	8
Home Contents	5	44	-	8	-
Home Building	5	42	-	7	-
Home Personal Effects	3	50	94	9	-
On Site Caravan	1	46	-	-	0
Touring Caravan	1	45	-	-	0
Boatsure	3	43	89	7	-
Motor Personal Accident	1	44	-	12	-
Legal Hassles (Legal)	3	43	-	12	-
What Can You Do (Car Theft)	2	44	91	-	-
What Thieves Cost You	3	45	-	-	-
Roundabouts version 1	2	43	-	4	1
Roundabouts version 2	9	50	-	6	2
Country Roads	9	44	35	-	0
Bus Priority	1	52	-	-	2
Sorry but You're Over The Limit	5	51	100	10	-
Don't Blow It	8	63	2	11	-
How Many Drinks	0	56	-	-	-
Children Crossing	8	54	92	-	0
S. Lanes	7	54	-	-	0
Keep Left	8	54	98	-	0

- indicates not applicable or not tested

Introduction

To determine the extent to which NRMA leaflets are read, a research study was conducted by the Publications Editor between November, 1985 and August, 1987.

The study covered leaflets which are distributed to members by direct means, such as bulk mail or magazine insert, and leaflets which are distributed to target audiences who have requested leaflets, or who may be members of special interest groups.

The intention of the study was to determine the extent of reading, and if appropriate and feasible, to determine why some leaflets may not be read as diligently as others.

The study covered 24 leaflets: twelve were product marketing oriented; twelve were community service. Some leaflets were excluded because of the mechanical difficulty in finding a target audience (third-party property damage is an example).

Some of the leaflets were in full color, some were one or two colors. All were of the standard NRMA dimensions—about 90 mm (3.5 inches) wide by 210 mm (8.25 inches) deep.

The study was conducted in Sydney suburbs, selected randomly, (except where special interest leaflets, such as on-site caravan and boat insurance, were considered.) These were studied in appropriate locations such as caravan parks and marine centers.

Total distribution of leaflets in the study was more than 15,000.

Method

To test leaflets delivered directly to members, leaflets were letter-box dropped in suburban locations, selected at random. A week later, houses where leaflets had been dropped were revisited, and a series of questions asked of householders to determine the extent of reading.

The study was confined to the responses of those who said they were NRMA members.

The sample size for each set of interviews was 250, however, a second check was made on each leaflet at a different location, with an apparently different socio-economic status, giving a total sample for each leaflet of 500.

The questions asked of the sample members referred to their NRMA membership—whether the leaflet had been read in part, in entirety, or not at all; whether the headline had been read, and if so, whether it had been understood; if the leaflet had not been read, the reasons for this; and whether the illustration on the leaflet had been recalled.

A series of questions also was asked about type size preferences. A sample of text in different type sizes was shown to each sample member, in an attempt to determine with which type sizes they felt comfortable, and to determine the optimum type size or sizes for the text of leaflets. Sample size for this part of the study was 4,000 (Figure 3).

The sample members were also asked if they had an interest in the subject strong enough for them to have requested information about it. This information was sought, in an attempt to differentiate between responses of members who had received the leaflet gratuitously (may not have been interested in, and probably would not have sought information on, the subject), and those who might have formed a target audience. Only those whose demonstrated interest in the subject was strong were included in the latter assessment (Figure 1).

To ensure this, target audiences, as far as possible, were sought from locations and groups where a specific interest might be apparent. For example, target audiences for a leaflet on school crossings were sought from parent groups; on home insurance from Neighborhood Watch groups; for boat insurance, at marine centers.

On advice from the Ogilvy Center for Research and Development, California, an attempt was made to validate the presumed target audience responses. In this, true targets were set up. NRMA members visiting branches were asked if they had any specific interests in community affairs matters, or in insurance or other products. Those who answered positively were asked if they would like to receive a leaflet on the subject, and if they would be prepared to be interviewed on the subject, after having received the leaflets.

A sufficient number agreed to form target samples for four leaflets—two product marketing, and two community service.

The analysis of responses was statistically similar to that resulting from those who had received leaflets mailed directly, but who had expressed considerable interest in the subject, and who indicated they would have become targets for further information. The variation of responses between the true target and supposed target groups was less than two percent plus or minus, which, given the sample size, is statistically insignificant.

Because of this, and because of the costly and difficult mechanics of targeting an audience for a single leaflet for research purposes, it was decided to proceed with the method of delivering leaflets directly, then separating the target audience from the general audience by interview.

Research

1. **Extent of reading**—There appeared to be little or no relationship between the length of words in a leaflet and the extent of reading. However, the format, typestyle, and type size were found to be significant:

   • A community service leaflet on *Roundabouts* was published in two editions: one of 400 words, and a later expanded edition of 500 words.

   When the leaflet was redesigned, stock was changed from a pale yellow to white, with pale blue tint areas. At the same time, the type style was changed from a sans serif face to a serif face. Previous research, in the U.S. and in Australia, into comprehension of type styles has shown serif type to be more readable, and more comfortable for readers than sans serif.

   The first edition of the *Roundabout* leaflet was read by 14 percent of readers; the second by 35 percent.

   • *Bus priority*, a 300-word leaflet on a changed traffic feature, was read by 20 percent of the target sample. *Keep Left Unless Overtaking*, a 250-word leaflet on another traffic change, was read by 34 percent. *Bus priority* was set in sans serif type; *Keep Left* was set in serif type.

- *Sorry But You're Over the Limit*, a 1000-word leaflet on drunk driving, was read by 34 percent of the sample. *How Many Drinks*, a 1000-word leaflet on a similar subject, was read by 8 percent. *Sorry But You're Over the Limit* had four pages to accommodate the 1000 words. For *How Many Drinks* the type size was reduced to accommodate the text on one page.

A question emerged: why do so many people request leaflets on a subject, then not read them?

The answers given to a series of questions asked in the study to determine this point indicate that, for those leaflets with readership below the average (25 percent):

- *41 percent said they were too busy;*

- *21 percent said they started to read, but didn't finish, and couldn't say why;*

- *9 percent said they didn't read, and didn't know why;*

- *8 percent said they tried, but found the leaflets not interesting enough;*

- *4 percent said they intended to read, but forgot to;*

- *17 percent had read the leaflets.*

This apparent failure of leaflets to attract readers from the target audience promoted a subsidiary study into the level of comprehension. The question emerged: is there something in the structure of the leaflets which inhibits reading, or turns readers off?

2. **Reader comprehension of leaflets:** Based on previous research, in Australia and overseas, judgements could be made about the design of leaflets with below average target readership.

All had one or more of three apparent defects: on some *the text was set in sans serif type*, which readers generally have difficulty with; *one was in what seemed to be unacceptably small type*; or their *design did not entice readers*.

The latter seems subjective. However, there is published research which demonstrates how people scan, react to, and read, marketing material. This research was conducted by the Institute for Direct Marketing in Munich, under Professor Siegfried Vogele. Dr. Vogele's study, using eye-camera techniques, and samples of several thousand readers, has shown, for example, that when readers open a marketing piece, such as a leaflet, their eyes take a specific scanning path through the text. Their eyes make fixations at headlines and illustrations, and these fixations help them to determine whether they will read the piece or not.

Many of the NRMA leaflets, which attracted low response from readers, do not have headlines on the inside pages to attract the reader's eye in the scanning task. According to Professor Vogele's research, these leaflets have less chance of being read than do leaflets which have a headline, placed appropriately, on the center spread. (A summary of Professor Vogele's ideas is contained at the end of this chapter.)

This NRMA study made no attempt to replicate the German research, the expertise and high-cost equipment not being available in Australia.

It was, however, possible to pursue the other two factors—design, and type style.

In this phase, the car theft campaign leaflet *What You Can Do*, was subjected to a test of comprehensibility using the Rehe Rate of Work Method. This is conducted by presenting the printed material to a random sample, and asking members of the sample to read the leaflet under supervision. After reading, the participants are asked a series of questions designed to test the level of their comprehension of the material. (This method was championed by Professor Rolf Rehe, Professor of Typography at Indiana University, and is widely accepted as a sound means of testing typographical elements in the field.)

The method is used when there is doubt about the validity of design or typography. In this instance, the continuous text of the leaflet tested was set in a sans serif face, which earlier research has shown to result in poor readability.

To provide a measure of control, the leaflet text was also reset in a serif type face, in identical format, and the two leaflets tested in parallel.

The sample size was 400, divided into two groups of 200. Each group was given one version of the leaflet. The sample was confined to NRMA members who said they had not previously read any of the material.

Good comprehension of the sans serif version was recorded by 22 percent of the sample, and fair comprehension by 37 percent of the sample.

(Good comprehension means that readers were able to comprehend at least two-thirds of the points made in the text sufficiently well to react to it; fair comprehension means that readers were able to comprehend between one-third and two-thirds; poor comprehension means that readers were able to comprehend less than one-third of the points made in the text.)

When the serif type leaflet was tested, 83 percent of readers showed good comprehension, and 9 percent fair comprehension.

These results were higher than recorded in published research into serif and sans serif body type, but in the earlier research, longer text material was used. However, the proportion of poor comprehension in sans serif versus serif setting, 5:1, was identical to that recorded in earlier research.

Results of this phase of the study were:

Comprehension levels			
	Good	**Fair**	**Poor**
Body matter set in sans serif	22	37	41
Body matter set in serif	83	9	8

3. Headlines: Half the people who receive leaflets say they read little or no further than the headlines.

The extent of headline reading seems in broad terms, constant, and is not conditional on the subject of the leaflet, its length in words, design, or distribution method.

However, the extent of headline reading shouldn't be taken to imply that headline readers have necessarily understood the leaflet's message.

To test this, an a priori judgement was made of the headlines of two leaflets on a similar theme, and additional questions were asked about them.

Table 1 shows percentage responses to the question: which type size or sizes do you find easy to read as continuous text?

Point Size	% Response	Point Size	% Response
8 point	14	12	72
8/9	21	12/13	90
8/10	26	12/14	82
9	63	13	66
9/10	66	13/14	70
9/11	71	13/15	68
10	69	14	59
10/11	86	14/15	61
10/12	92	14/16	63
11	77	15	21
11/12	93	15/16	25
11/13	98	15/17	28

Table 2 shows percentage responses to the question: which type size do you find most comfortable to read as continuous text? Some sample members were unable to choose between two styles.

Point Size	% Response
10/11	6
10/12	19
11	2
11/12	14
11/13	25
12	7
12/13	18
12 on 14	9

Figure 3.
Sample of reader responses to different size text.

While 62 percent of the sample read only the headline of a leaflet headed *Don't Blow It*, only 4 percent of them could explain accurately what the headline conveyed.

On the other hand, of the 50 percent of the sample who read the headline *Sorry But You're Over the Limit*, all understood what the headline conveyed, and therefore had absorbed the message to a considerable degree without reading the text. It is possible that in this instance the cover illustration reinforced the message of the headline. However, further tests showed similar responses to leaflets on insurance and traffic conditions, where illustrations were not a factor (Figure 1), and when leaflets were distributed gratuitously (Figure 2).

Sample members said the subheadings indicating insurance portfolio helped them to understand the main headline on the front of most, but not all, insurance leaflets. Exceptions were the new edition of the car insurance leaflet, *Is This the End for Ostrich Insurance*, which most readers, found to be obscure, and the Life Savings Bonds leaflets, *There's Got to Be an Easier Way of Investing*, which readers said they found confusing, and on which the portfolio title was obscured by the illustration.

4. **Illustrations:** Readers recall photographs much more easily than they recall line illustrations or diagrams (Figure 1).

Although no research study has yet forged a link between recall and intention to buy or act, it is clear that illustrations can be used to support a message. If a photograph contains an element of the message, rather than being mere decoration, it's reasonable to infer that the photograph helps to reinforce the message contained in the headline or text.

Moreover, the research conducted by the Institute for Direct Marketing in Munich, cited earlier in this chapter, has shown that illustrations can help to influence a reader's decision to read or not to read.

5. **Size of text type:** Parallel to the main part of the study, a measure was made of ease of reading and readers' preference in type size for continuous text.

More than 75 percent of readers found type within the range of 10 point on an 11 point body to 12 point on a 14 point body easy to read (Figure 3, Table 1.)

The most preferred type sizes were 11 point on a 13 point body (preferred by 25 percent of the sample), 10 on 12 point (preferred by 19 percent), and 12 on 13 point (preferred by 18 percent) (Figure 3, Table 2).

Readers made a clear distinction between type set natural, with which they said they did not feel comfortable, and type set with one point or two points interlinear space, with which generally they felt comfortable. The distinction between one and two points space was not so clear in readers' eyes, but a heavy majority opted for two point spacing as the most comfortable.

The white "river" created by extra spacing provides an eye channel for the reader to find the next line.

It was noticed that practiced readers found type with one point interlinear spacing to be adequate; most readers, however, are not skilful, and prefer two point spacing to enable them to decipher text with ease.

Table 1 in Figure 3 shows an extreme drop in reading comfort when type is below 9 points. The leaflet *How Many Drinks*, which registered badly in the study into the extent of reading, was set in a type size about 8 points.

Relative type sizes are shown in Appendix A.

6. **Distribution method:** The low readership of leaflets distributed directly must place in question the economic validity of this type of distribution for informational material.

The average readership of leaflets distributed to members gratuitously was 5 percent—the best result was 9 percent, the worst less than 1 percent.

This reponse may be acceptable when, say, a million leaflets are distributed, or when sales can be used to allay costs.

A response of 5 percent with a distribution of one million would give a readership of 50,000, which may be considered satisfactory to engender sales.

But when distribution is only 50,000, readership at 5 percent becomes 2,500—at a proportionately higher effective unit cost.

During NRMA's anti-theft campaign, the leaflet *What Thieves Cost You* was distributed as an insert in *The Open Road* magazine, with a total delivery of 900,000 in the Sydney Metropolitan area.

Following distribution of the magazine, a study was made of the extent of readership of the leaflet from this method of delivery.

Of a separate sample of 600 readers in a variety of suburbs and locations, 4 percent said they had read the leaflet. Thirteen of the 600 said they had sought more information. If this response is extrapolated to the total delivery, it means a response from 19,500 members to the leaflet drop.

Summary of Professor Vogele's research

In a direct marketing piece, which could include a letter, leaflet, response card and envelope, Professor Vogele has performed detailed studies. A number of major points have come out of the studies. For example, the average time spent in reviewing the contents of an envelope was less than 12 seconds. If it was not of interest, it was then thrown away.

In designing a leaflet, important considerations are as follows:

- People will review the cover first. Approximately half will then open the center spread, while half will go to the back cover.

- Copy is not read at first, but quickly scanned, with only photographs and major headlines taken in.

- In the center pages, most people will start at the right-hand page and scan back towards the center. Eye-catching illustrations on the left-hand page will bring the reader's attention over to the left.

- Large, powerful illustrations should not be on the lower right center page. This will have the effect of drawing the reader's attention immediately to the bottom right-hand corner and then out of the page.

- Color pictures are more appealing than monochrome. Therefore place color pictures to the left of center spread, with black and white pictures to the right.

- People pictures are looked at before product pictures. Therefore, place pictures of people to the left of center spread, with product pictures to the right.

- Star bursts have only limited appeal. They draw attention to their contents, but also tend to attract a person's attention away from the important text copy.

- Shorter sentences and shorter paragraphs get better attention than longer ones.

- Vertical shapes are preferred to horizontal shapes by a large percentage. A diagonal shape is even better.

- Larger pictures are more appealing than smaller ones.

- A sequence of pictures will be noted before individual pictures.

- Action pictures will get attention before still pictures.

- Portraits get looked at before full length pictures.

- Children get attention before adults.

To get the best possible response to a direct mail posting, a direct response option should be included. A separate reply card rates up to a three times better response than a coupon torn off the basic leaflet.

To encourage better response, include the prospect's name on the response card, and also include a contact name in the return mail address.

A separate letter should be enclosed with the leaflet and response card. Eye camera studies have shown that recipients peruse the letter starting from the top, quickly noting any highlighted points in the letter, moving to the signature, and then any P.S. under the signature.

A minimum number of benefits should be highlighted in the letter by using underlining, bolding, or color. A hard-to-understand signature at the bottom can be a turn-off.

Recommendations

1. We should heed published research into how and why readers react to printed material in all its forms—unpalatable though that research may sometimes be to our aesthetic senses.

   There seems little point, for example, in setting body text in sans serif type because it looks clean, modern, precise, or progressive, when all the evidence points to its being unacceptable to readers as continuous text.

   We should ensure, instead, that our leaflet design and contents accommodate known reading traits and idiosyncrasies, rather than ignore them.

2. The extent of headline reading among readers gives us an opportunity to make our messages understood. David Ogilvy, in his book *Confessions of an Advertising Man,* says that five times as many readers read an advertising headline as read the remainder of the copy, and this research also shows a great disparity between headline and text reading.

   Headlines should contain enough of the message to stand on their own—as they frequently have to do.

   Teasing or intriguing headlines, unless they contain the message, may fail.

3. Where possible, leaflets should contain illustrations and a headline, on both cover and inside pages to support the message, and entice the reader to read rather than merely scan.

4. We should consider the validity of randomly distributed leaflets, measuring the expected rewards against the cost. The escalating cost of printing may make an average readership of one in twenty, less than economically acceptable.

Appendix A

8 point on 8 point body

Photocomposition contributes a great deal to the revival of fine type design through its ability to restore artistry and craftmanship in a form practical for the fast machine-set speed. And only the designer's material - his palette - has changed. Where the designer punch-cutter cut his original letter to size in metal, the photoletter design is drawn larger on white paper which is then mounted onto a black background and hand-cut. It is then photographically reduced to master type size.

8 point on 9 point body

Photocomposition contributes a great deal to the revival of fine type design through its ability to restore artistry and craftmanship in a form practical for the fast machine-set speed. And only the designer's material - his palette - has changed. Where the designer punch-cutter cut his original letter to size in metal, the photoletter design is drawn larger on white paper which is then mounted onto a black background and hand-cut. It is then photographically reduced to master type size.

8 point on 10 point body

Photocomposition contributes a great deal to the revival of fine type design through its ability to restore artistry and craftmanship in a form practical for the fast machine-set speed. And only the designer's material - his palette - has changed. Where the designer punch-cutter cut his original letter to size in metal, the photoletter design is drawn larger on white paper which is then mounted onto a black background and hand-cut. It is then photographically reduced to master type size.

9 point on 9 point body

Photocomposition contributes a great deal to the revival of fine type design through its ability to restore artistry and craftmanship in a form practical for the fast machine-set speed. And only the designer's material - his palette - has changed. Where the designer punch-cutter cut his original letter to size in metal, the photoletter design is drawn larger on white paper which is then mounted onto a black background and hand-cut. It is then photographically reduced to master type size.

9 point on 10 point body

Photocomposition contributes a great deal to the revival of fine type design through its ability to restore artistry and craftmanship in a form practical for the fast machine-set speed. And only the designer's material - his palette - has changed. Where the designer punch-cutter cut his original letter to size in metal, the photoletter design is drawn larger on white paper which is then mounted onto a black background and hand-cut. It is then photographically reduced to master type size.

9 point on 11 point body

Photocomposition contributes a great deal to the revival of fine type design through its ability to restore artistry and craftmanship in a form practical for the fast machine-set speed. And only the designer's material - his palette - has changed. Where the designer punch-cutter cut his original letter to size in metal, the photoletter design is drawn larger on white paper which is then mounted onto a black background and hand-cut. It is then photographically reduced to master type size.

10 point on 10 point body

Photocomposition contributes a great deal to the revival of fine type design through its ability to restore artistry and craftmanship in a form practical for the fast machine-set speed. And only the designer's material - his palette - has changed. Where the designer punch-cutter cut his original letter to size in metal, the photoletter design is drawn larger on white paper which is then mounted onto a black background and hand-cut. It is then photographically reduced to master type size.

10 point on 11 point body

Photocomposition contributes a great deal to the revival of fine type design through its ability to restore artistry and craftmanship in a form practical for the fast machine-set speed. And only the designer's material - his palette - has changed. Where the designer punch-cutter cut his original letter to size in metal, the photoletter design is drawn larger on white paper which is then mounted onto a black background and hand-cut. It is then photographically reduced to master type size.

10 point on 12 point body

Photocomposition contributes a great deal to the revival of fine type design through its ability to restore artistry and craftmanship in a form practical for the fast machine-set speed. And only the designer's material - his palette - has changed. Where the designer punch-cutter cut his original letter to size in metal, the photoletter design is drawn larger on white paper which is then mounted onto a black background and hand-cut. It is then photographically reduced to master type size.

11 point on 11 point body

Photocomposition contributes a great deal to the revival of fine type design through its ability to restore artistry and craftmanship in a form practical for the fast machine-set speed. And only the designer's material - his palette - has changed. Where the designer punch-cutter cut his original letter to size in metal, the photoletter design is drawn larger on white paper which is then mounted onto a black background and hand-cut. It is then photographically reduced to master type size.

11 point on 12 point body

Photocomposition contributes a great deal to the revival of fine type design through its ability to restore artistry and craftmanship in a form practical for the fast machine-set speed. And only the designer's material - his palette - has changed. Where the designer punch-cutter cut his original letter to size in metal, the photoletter design is drawn larger on white paper which is then mounted onto a black background and hand-cut. It is then photographically reduced to master type size.

11 point on 13 point body

Photocomposition contributes a great deal to the revival of fine type design through its ability to restore artistry and craftmanship in a form practical for the fast machine-set speed. And only the designer's material - his palette - has changed. Where the designer punch-cutter cut his original letter to size in metal, the photoletter design is drawn larger on white paper which is then mounted onto a black background and hand-cut. It is then photographically reduced to master type size.

12 point on 12 point body

Photocomposition contributes a great deal to the revival of fine type design through its ability to restore artistry and craftmanship in a form practical for the fast machine-set speed. And only the designer's material - his palette - has changed. Where the designer punch-cutter cut his original letter to size in metal, the photoletter design is drawn larger on white paper which is then mounted onto a black background and hand-cut. It is then photographically reduced to master type size.

12 point on 13 point body

Photocomposition contributes a great deal to the revival of fine type design through its ability to restore artistry and craftmanship in a form practical for the fast machine-set speed. And only the designer's material - his palette - has changed. Where the designer punch-cutter cut his original letter to size in metal, the photoletter design is drawn larger on white paper which is then mounted onto a black background and hand-cut. It is then photographically reduced to master type size.

12 point on 14 point body

Photocomposition contributes a great deal to the revival of fine type design through its ability to restore artistry and craftmanship in a form practical for the fast machine-set speed. And only the designer's material - his palette - has changed. Where the designer punch-cutter cut his original letter to size in metal, the photoletter design is drawn larger on white paper which is then mounted onto a black background and hand-cut. It is then photographically reduced to master type size.

13 point on 13 point body

Photocomposition contributes a great deal to the revival of fine type design through its ability to restore artistry and craftmanship in a form practical for the fast machine-set speed. And only the designer's material - his palette - has changed. Where the designer punch-cutter cut his original letter to size in metal, the photoletter design is drawn larger on white paper which is then mounted onto a black background and hand-cut. It is then photographically reduced to master type size.

13 point on 14 point body

Photocomposition contributes a great deal to the revival of fine type design through its ability to restore artistry and craftmanship in a form practical for the fast machine-set speed. And only the designer's material - his palette - has changed. Where the designer punch-cutter cut his original letter to size in metal, the photoletter design is drawn larger on white paper which is then mounted onto a black background and hand-cut. It is then photographically reduced to master type size.

13 point on 15 point body

Photocomposition contributes a great deal to the revival of fine type design through its ability to restore artistry and craftmanship in a form practical for the fast machine-set speed. And only the designer's material - his palette - has changed. Where the designer punch-cutter cut his original letter to size in metal, the photoletter design is drawn larger on white paper which is then mounted onto a black background and hand-cut. It is then photographically reduced to master type size.

14 point on 14 point body

Photocomposition contributes a great deal to the revival of fine type design through its ability to restore artistry and craftmanship in a form practical for the fast machine-set speed. And only the designer's material - his palette - has changed. Where the designer punch-cutter cut his original letter to size in metal, the photoletter design is drawn larger on white paper which is then mounted onto a black background and hand-cut. It is then photographically reduced to master type size.

14 point on 15 point body

Photocomposition contributes a great deal to the revival of fine type design through its ability to restore artistry and craftmanship in a form practical for the fast machine-set speed. And only the designer's material - his palette - has changed. Where the designer punch-cutter cut his original letter to size in metal, the photoletter design is drawn larger on white paper which is then mounted onto a black background and hand-cut. It is then photographically reduced to master type size.

14 point on 16 point body

Photocomposition contributes a great deal to the revival of fine type design through its ability to restore artistry and craftmanship in a form practical for the fast machine-set speed. And only the designer's material - his palette - has changed. Where the designer punch-cutter cut his original letter to size in metal, the photoletter design is drawn larger on white paper which is then mounted onto a black background and hand-cut. It is then photographically reduced to master type size.

15 point on 15 point body

Photocomposition contributes a great deal to the revival of fine type design through its ability to restore artistry and craftmanship in a form practical for the fast machine-set speed. And only the designer's material - his palette - has changed. Where the designer punch-cutter cut his original letter to size in metal, the photoletter design is drawn larger on white paper which is then mounted onto a black background and hand-cut. It is then photographically reduced to master type size.

15 point on 16 point body

Photocomposition contributes a great deal to the revival of fine type design through its ability to restore artistry and craftmanship in a form practical for the fast machine-set speed. And only the designer's material - his palette - has changed. Where the designer punch-cutter cut his original letter to size in metal, the photoletter design is drawn larger on white paper which is then mounted onto a black background and hand-cut. It is then photographically reduced to master type size.

15 point on 17 point body

Photocomposition contributes a great deal to the revival of fine type design through its ability to restore artistry and craftmanship in a form practical for the fast machine-set speed. And only the designer's material - his palette - has changed. Where the designer punch-cutter cut his original letter to size in metal, the photoletter design is drawn larger on white paper which is then mounted onto a black background and hand-cut. It is then photographically reduced to mast

About the Authors

Tony Webster

Barbara Larter

Tony Webster has worked in the computer industry for over twenty years and in the publishing industry for over ten. He is the author of the popular book *Microcomputer Buyer's Guide* and was the winner of the 1986 McGraw-Hill award for Distinquished Achievement in New Product Development for his work in publishing.

Barbara Larter has remained at the forefront of the desktop publishing industry since its inception. She has used this medium in the design and layout of technical manuals and promotional material. Ms. Larter joined Webster and Associates to research and develop training material specifically for the desktop publishing industry.

Index

A

Adobe 69, 72
Advertising 7, 43, 59, 61, 63, 183, 217, 228, 229, 237, 269
Advertisement 13, 14, 44, 62, 183, 217, 235-39
Analogous harmony 231
Annual reports 14
Automated offset 250
Axis of orientation 4, 7

B

Balance 115-17, 119, 209, 211-13
Benefits 13, 148, 149, 151, 152, 268
Bibliographic details 189, 191
Bitstream fontware 72–6
Bleeding 211, 212, 247
Body text 25, 32, 56, 58, 64, 66, 89, 90, 92, 95, 96, 121, 142, 190, 193, 197–9, 203, 221, 242, 269
Body type 57, 58, 59, 61, 64, 90
Border 22, 154, 183–6, 240, 211–13, 249
Bullets 148, 149, 151, 152, 155

C

Capitals 41-3, 48-58, 62, 241
Captions 22, 26, 63, 90-5, 122, 149, 190
Centered 60, 190, 192, 209
Color 19, 22, 115, 148, 183, 211, 217–33, 240, 246-8, 250, 267, 268
Commercial printers 250

Complementary

Complementary harmony 231
Comprehension 13, 43, 44, 46, 56-9, 61, 65, 90, 94, 156, 175, 217, 219-30, 240, 242, 261-64
Condensing 45, 48, 49
Contents 34, 189–92, 267
Contrast 109, 112
Conventional design 209
Conventional publishing 8–10
Copy fitting 27
CorelDRAW 178
Cropping 245

D

Design 3, 8, 15, 21, 31, 43, 63, 103, 112, 115, 125, 148, 168, 209–13, 235, 254
Desktop publishing 3, 8, 20, 27, 39, 45, 73, 125
Direct mail 268
Distribution method 265–6
Drop in 246
Dummy 21, 28, 29, 31, 100, 247, 249
Dummy chapter 21, 28, 29

E

Editorial 44
Estimate 249
Eye camera 268

F

Field 167
Film 246

Focal point 167, 168
Folding 248–9
Foreword 189, 190
Freedom 213
Fringe 167, 168
Full color 246

G

Glossary 191
Golden proportion 103, 104
Graphics 19, 27, 30, 89, 90, 109, 148,
    171, 172, 177, 178, 180, 183-6
Grip 247
Gutenberg Diagram 4–6

H

Harmony 13, 104, 109-11, 209
    211, 233
Headline 13, 15, 26, 29, 39, 41-53, 56,
    58, 62-4, 91-4, 123, 125, 159-61,
    163, 167, 211, 218–221, 235-44,
    254-6, 261, 262, 264, 267, 269
High chroma 218-20
Horizontal 22, 43, 64, 103, 115,
    148, 154, 268
Horizontal rules 211

I

Illustrations 9, 10, 13, 14, 26, 43, 64,
    109, 111, 112, 115, 159, 175, 211,
    235, 237, 256, 261, 264, 267, 269
Images 171, 180, 245
Index 189, 191, 193
Instant Printers 249
Interleaving 248
ISBN 190, 195, 200

J

Job 245, 247, 248–50
Jumps 61, 63
Justified 35, 39-40, 59-61, 92, 94–6,
    199, 237

K

Kerning 45, 46, 48, 58, 163

L

Leading 27, 67, 68, 197, 199
Leaflets 253–69
Line bromides 245
Line length 58
Long publications 194, 197
Low chroma 220, 221
Lowercase 41, 43, 48-58, 62, 95,
    96, 148, 151, 152, 192, 237, 238

M

Manuals 14, 192-4, 197
Master chapter 28-30, 141, 143
Masthead 26, 28, 33, 34, 39-40,
    93, 95, 96, 98, 100, 248
Mechanicals 245
Modern design 209–13
Monochromatic harmony 231
Motion 209, 211, 213

N

Newsletters 3, 9, 13, 14, 16, 19, 26,
    28-33, 39, 40, 43, 89, 91-8, 100,
    115, 119-22, 125, 128, 129, 245,
    249

O

Oblong, 103
      Regular 103
      Golden 103
Ogilvy Center 258
Operator manuals 14
Optical center 118
Ornamental 39
Overhead transparencies 147-9, 51, 55, 56

P

PageMaker 20, 22, 27, 28, 65-70, 73, 91-6, 120, 124, 125, 128, 148, 161, 171, 172, 177, 178, 180, 184-6, 189, 193, 194, 196, 199, 205, 245
Paper,
      Matt 221
      Gloss 221
PC Paintbrush 177, 180
Pictures 19, 22, 26, 27, 92, 96, 122, 126, 128, 178, 191, 211, 245, 267, 268
Planning 19
Plate making 246
PMS number 246
Pointing devices 168, 171, 172, 209
PostScript 65-70, 73, 74, 172, 178-80
Preface 189, 190, 191
Press release 13, 15, 139-44
Primary Optical Area 4, 7
Printer fonts 74
Proportion 103
Pyramid 159

R

Ragged left 59-61
Ragged right 59-61, 94
Reading gravity 4, 7
Reading patterns 4, 236

Reading rhythm 4, 7
Rehe, Professor Rolf 261
Reverse 58, 61, 177, 190, 191, 228–9, 242
Roman 39, 40, 42, 43, 46, 48, 58, 61, 70–2, 75, 76, 104, 190, 210, 220, 230
Rules 183, 184
Running the job 247

S

Sans serif 26, 39, 40, 42, 43, 46, 49, 56, 57, 61, 65-9, 89, 104, 148, 210, 220, 229, 259–62, 269
Scoring 248
Screen fonts 74
Screen wash out 247
Screen bromides 245
Script 39
Serif 26, 39, 40, 46, 49, 56-8, 62, 65-9, 89, 94, 95, 148, 197, 210, 237, 259, 261, 262
Shapes, 22, 103, 105, 175, 213, 241
      vertical 211
      horizontal 211
      diagonal 211
Shells 249
Spot color 217, 220, 240, 246, 247, 248
Square serif 39, 42, 43
Star 167
Star bursts 267
Stitching 248–9
Stock 246
Strip in 246

T

Table of contents 189, 190
Target audience 13, 41, 253, 257-60
Terminal Anchor 4
Thumbnail sketches 20, 21, 167, 235
Tinted text 223–7
Title page 189, 190, 199

To fit 246
Trimming 248
Turnaround 247
Typeface 40, 66, 73-5, 77, 190, 210
Type family 40
Type font 23, 27, 40, 112

V

Vertical 22, 24, 58, 103, 209, 211,
    213, 268
Vertical rules 24, 33, 90, 211
Vogele, Professor Siegfried 261, 267–
    68

W

Wash-up 248
Wet 248
Widows 61, 62
Word processing 27, 28, 39
WYSIWYG 26

More Management and Business Resources from M&T Books

PageMaker 3 By Example

by David Webster and Tony Webster

PageMaker 3 By Example is an excellent hands-on tutorial designed to make this versatile program easy to understand and use. Its contents are based on over 1,000 hours of training users on desktop publishing.

The book is broken up into modules with each progressive module covering more detailed operations of PageMaker. You'll find numerous examples of how different concepts are utilized. Topics include loading files, manipulating PageMaker text blocks, text editing, internal graphics, advanced picture formatting, templates, setting defaults, printing, and much more.

Book only (PC version)	*Item #050-8*	*$22.95*
Book only (Macintosh version)	*Item # 049-4*	*$22.95*

Dr. Dobb's Essential HyperTalk Handbook

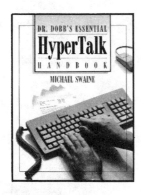

by Michael Swaine

Michael Swaine, well-known columnist and editor-at-large of *Dr. Dobb's Journal*, provides a complete analysis of HyperTalk. Rapidly gaining popularity among both long-time programmers and novices, HyperTalk is a powerful programming language that can be used to develop serious applications while remaining appropriate for use by less experienced users. Solid examples and analyses are given. A handy technical reference section is included in addition to a Programmer's Peg Board full of programs and utilities that will orient programmers to the environment. Topics such as the move from authoring to scripting, concepts and components of the language, programming style considerations, and much more are presented. Programs are available on disk.

Book & Disk (Macintosh)	*Item #99-2*	*$39.95*
Book only	*Item #98-4*	*$24.95*

More Resources ...

Dynamics of Desktop Publishing Design

by Tony Webster and Barbara Larter

Dynamics of Desktop Publishing Design is the result of extensive research in the field of typography (the craft of designing communications using desktop publishing technology). The authors demonstrate design and layout principles to help you communicate your message more effectively in printed pieces. Some of the topics include: type styles, headlines, proportion, tone harmony, contrast, and directing eye movement. Examples and guidelines are given for every type of document, from newletters and books to press releases and overhead transparencies.
Many of the concepts are further emphasized in hands-on tutorials designed for PageMaker 3.

Book only   *Item #051-6*   *$22.95*

To Order: Return this form with your payment to: **M&T Books**, 501 Galveston Drive, Redwood City, CA 94063 or **CALL TOLL-FREE 1-800-533-4372** Mon-Fri 8AM-5PM Pacific Standard Time (in California, call 1-800-356-2002).

☐ **YES!** Please send me the following: ☐ Check enclosed, payable to **M&T Books**.

Item#	Description	Disk	Price

Charge my ☐ Visa ☐ MC ☐ AmEx

Card No. _____

Exp. Date _____

Signature _____

Name _____

Address _____

City _____

State _____ Zip _____

Subtotal _____

CA residents add sales tax __ % _____

Add $2.99 per item for shipping

and handling _____

TOTAL _____

7033

M&T BOOKS